CALL TO LOVE

CALL TO LOVE

David Beresford

Brookscraft Publishing

CALL TO LOVE

Published 2026 by:
Brookscraft Publishing
Buffalo, New York 14203
info@brookscraftpublishing
https://brookscraftpublishing.com

First published in 2023 by Cedar Tree Books.

ISBN: 978-1-969682-36-0 EBOOK
ISBN: 978-1-969682-37-7 PAPERBACK
ISBN: 978-1-969682-38-4 HARDCOVER

Title: Call to Love
Author: David Beresford
Editor: Nick Cerchio
Book Design: Bob Schwartz
Cover image: soft_light/shutterstock.com
Copyright: © 2023 David Beresford

Unless otherwise noted, Scripture quotations are from:

The New Revised Standard Version Bible (NRSV)
©1989 National Council of the Churches of Christ in the United States of America.
Used with permission.

The Revised New Jerusalem Bible (RNJB)
©2019 by Henry Wansbrough.
Used with permission.

Printed and bound in the United States of America

Dedication

To Ruth

What most truly makes a man a man, at the fine point of his being and the root of his personality, is his capacity for loving, for loving to the uttermost, for giving himself in a love which is stronger than death and which reaches out into eternity.

Pope Paul VI
October 25, 1970

Table of Contents

Foreword

When Jesus gathered with his disciples the night before his crucifixion, he gave them the most effective and powerful tool they would need for the work entrusted to their care for the rest of their lives—the *mandatum novum*, the "new command." What was that command? Really just one word—love. Jesus would go on to say of all those ways others might know one was a follower of Jesus, the practice of love would trump them all. "By this," he said, "everyone will know you are my disciples," (John 13:35)

David Beresford's wonderful book, *Call to Love*, is a superb handbook that puts layer upon layer of flesh on Jesus' gift of love. Using the Holy Scriptures, stories from our Judeo-Christian tradition, and characters from his own tenure as a priest in God's Church, Beresford's work provides a rich tapestry that will help his readers understand more fully not only the spiritual disciplines but also how the practice of those disciplines empowers God's children to do the work He has given them to do.

Historians have been fascinated over the eons of time with the explosive growth of the Christian movement in its earliest days, from a precious few to untold numbers that eventually contributed to the collapse of a Roman Empire corrupted by its pagan principles. And, many of those same historians have found the primary armament in the arsenal of the follower of Jesus was active love. No philosophy, no movement—no group of followers loved as Jesus' followers loved.

Beresford's book is well-timed, for we live in a day and age that seems full of conflict and strife. *Call to Love* and the wisdom therein reminds us of a better way—the best way, to step from darkness to light and from despair to hope. Indeed, Jesus showed us that way— in the words of the great hymn by Peter Scholtes,

"They will know we are Christians by our love… by our love." This is, indeed a book for our age. The Church, and our hurting and broken world, will gain much from not only reading these pages but by putting them into practice. As Beresford reminds us—not just some, but all are called by God (p. 29). As we, individually and collectively, respond to that call with a hearty "yes," we will do the bidding of our Lord and live into the greatest of all commands—to love, one another. Read on… and, by God's grace and power—love all He sends your way, and therein reveals that you are—indeed, a disciple of Jesus!

The Reverend Russell J. Levenson, Jr., D.Min., D.D., OStJ
Rector, St. Martin's Episcopal Church, Houston, Texas

Preface

Two years ago I served as interim rector at St. Martha's, Bethany Beach, Delaware. In the summer, following the Sunday Eucharists, I would make the two-hour journey home to Wilmington. Passing the Blue Coast Seafood Grill on my left, and seeing the Indian River Bridge looming ahead, I would call Elsa, one of my parishioners.

Elsa was in charge of the pastoral care team and she knew who, among the congregation, needed a prayer, a visit, or a phone call, (or all three). I'm not sure if Elsa ever considered her work of pastoral ministry in terms of a "calling". She certainly had a love for the people she spoke to, and was always positive and sympathetic. Along with the phone calls, she and her wife Carol bought and delivered groceries to those who were housebound, and provided car rides to those who wanted them. Elsa offered her gifts to the church and served God through her ministry.

A church functions properly when all of its members are engaged in serving one another. There are those who, like Elsa, reach out to others in need. Then there are the musicians, vestry, church administrator, treasurer, altar guild, property team, flower guild, technicians, prayer circle, greeters, ushers, and more. There are many ways one can be useful within a church, and each area of service, however unexceptional, can be thought of as a calling.

This is a book about being called by God. It does not attempt to answer every question about "calling", but instead focuses on those whom God calls. The book contrasts the callings of people from the Bible with the callings of people I have known personally. What do their lives and experiences have to teach us? Why does God call us, and how should we respond? What are the similarities (and differences) between the lives of Bible people and the lives of people today?

The Bible contains many examples of men and women whom God calls. The main part of this book considers six of them: Jacob,

Moses, Samuel, Judith, Samson, and Mary, the mother of Jesus. I consider what their callings have in common, and explain how each call is unique. I have attempted to come at each person from a different angle. With Jacob, I have undertaken a psychological study. With Moses, I was inspired by a poem of David Whyte's. A famous fresco by Fra Angelico prompted my meditation on Mary.

In the last section of the book, there are profiles of four people I have known personally. They have, in their own way, responded to God's call. I have recounted their stories as straightforwardly as possible.

I wish Elsa were alive to read this book. She died towards the end of my tenure at St. Martha's. At her funeral, I quoted St. Teresa of Avila, who said, "Christ has no body but ours, no hands, no feet on earth but ours; ours are the eyes with which He looks compassion on this world." Elsa had a calling to serve, as do we all. She understood that when we turn our lives over to Christ, God will use what gifts we can offer for the sake of the kingdom of heaven.

God continues to seek people to share in his loving and healing work. I hope this book will encourage you to offer yourself to Christ, as you listen for God's voice in your own life. May it inspire you to respond in faith and love to God's call.

David Beresford
August 2023

Acknowledgments

Once again, I am indebted to Cedar Tree Books: to Nick, my publisher, whose friendship and encouragement have been instrumental in bringing this book to fruition. Thanks too, to Bob, the designer, who came up with the idea for the cover and has worked patiently and diligently to assemble the various parts of the book.

My wife Ruth, to whom this book is dedicated, has made suggestions that have helped to sharpen and clarify some of the text. In particular, she is responsible for persuading me to abandon my initial "two books in one" idea and focus instead on the one theme of "calling". As a result, I ended up exploring this subject in far greater detail than initially planned. For her critical advice, I am extremely grateful.

In writing a spiritual book, I acknowledge that God has been my helper. As in sermon writing, the Holy Spirit has had a significant input in the book's creation. Writing and revising is sometimes like rubbing a frosted window until you can see clearly through it. As a result, I hope the book's message is clear, and that it will provide both encouragement and enjoyment for the reader.

CALL TO LOVE

Part I
Hearing God's Call

CHAPTER 1

Call to Love

Jesus saw James and John…mending their nets, and he called them.
(Matthew 4:21)

E arly in the gospel accounts, Jesus calls a group of followers—ordinary men and women—to journey with him throughout the regions of Judaea, Samaria, Galilee, and beyond. As Jesus travels from village to town, he heals the sick and drives out demons. He teaches about the kingdom of heaven and encourages the people, through the use of parables, to discover the kingdom for themselves.

Gradually, his words begin to take root in the hearts and minds of those who knew him.

After Jesus' resurrection and ascension, some of the disciples reflected on the impact that Jesus had made to their lives. The writer of the letter to the Hebrews, for example, considered how Jesus' call was a fulfillment of an earlier call that God had made to his people, through the prophets.

Long ago God spoke to our ancestors in many and various ways by the prophets, but in these last days he has spoken to us by a Son, whom he appointed heir of all things, through whom he also created the worlds.

(Hebrews 1:1-2)

This opening sentence is almost a microcosm of the whole of the Bible. God, who once spoke to a nation, Israel, now speaks to all people through Jesus Christ. God reveals his plan for humanity through the prophets, who hear God's call and bear witness to the presence of God in their own lives and in the life of the nation. In one sense, Jesus is the last and most important of God's prophets.

God also speaks through poetry, wisdom, history, and the law. God speaks to us at all times and in all places. Yet if this call is continuous and all-pervasive, how do we discern it and how should we respond? Those are the questions that this book seeks to answer.

In the gospel of Matthew, Jesus calls four fishermen—Simon, Andrew, James, and John—to follow him. (Matthew 4:18-21) Jesus will expect them to make radical changes to their lives. Simon and Andrew, after Jesus called them, "left their nets and followed him." (Matthew 4:20) For these disciples, their first response was to let go of their nets. They were, in effect, letting go of what they were— fishermen—in order to become what God was calling them to be. The first call was a transition from *doing* to *being*. Later, their identity as Christians—as carriers of the Holy Spirit of God—would determine, to a large extent, what they would do.

By following Jesus, his followers were consenting to being transformed spiritually. To follow Jesus meant to be like him—a person of prayer, rich in love and compassion. Jesus is driven by his mission, which is to proclaim the kingdom of heaven. Jesus embodies two aspects of the spiritual and religious life: the *contemplative* and the *active*.

Jesus teaches wherever he goes, healing the sick, raising the dead, and forgiving sins. Ultimately, we see him submit his own will of his Father in heaven. To be like Jesus means to trust God as much as Jesus trusted his Father: that is, with complete confidence.

What motivates and energizes this work of healing and salvation is love. In his own life, Jesus personifies love in action. It is a way of life he shares with others, and the reason he calls the disciples is to teach them, equip them, bless them, and send them out to spread the gospel of Christ. Each of the disciples is called by name into a special kind of service built upon a close and loving relationship with Jesus. For each follower, it is a call to love.

Duccio di Buoninsegna, *The Calling of the Apostles Peter and Andrew*, c. 1308 - 1311, tempera on panel, 16 13/16 × 17 15/16 in., Samuel H. Kress Collection, National Gallery of Art, Washington, D.C.

CHAPTER 2

Faith

All things can be done for the one who believes.

(Mark 9:23)

To grow into the "full stature of Christ" (Ephesians 4:13) means embracing the life of faith. The disciples' faith grew from their close relationship with Jesus. They traveled with him across the plains and mountains of Palestine, observing him closely. Their faith grew because they were willing to ask questions, even if, at times, their questions exasperated Jesus. For them, conversion was not a single moment but an ongoing quest. The disciples were learning about the spiritual life from its source.

This continues to be true for us today. If we want to follow Christ, we must draw close to Jesus, and understand faith in terms of a conversion—not an overnight one, but of a gradual awakening and growing into the spiritual life.

Faith, in itself, is not confined to a belief in God. Actually, faith is everywhere. For example, I have faith that my mechanic will correctly fit new brakes to my car. When I go for a sponsored bike ride, I have faith that, if you have pledged money, at the end of the ride you will pay me. A trapeze artist will have faith that her partner will catch her as she completes her somersault.

Faith is sharpened by questions: "Isn't God an invention of human beings, to make their lives more bearable? Why does God allow suffering in the world? Hasn't science disproved that God exists?" Such questions are two-edged: they can lead people away from God, as well as to him. In the kind of world we want for ourselves, there may be no room for God. For those intent on pursuing their own goals and dreams, God can easily become a distraction. Sometimes there are questions about God that have no definitive answer. For this reason, there is always the temptation to stop asking questions and end the journey. One of the first lessons for a person of faith is to persevere, despite not knowing all the answers.

Faith requires an intention to discover the truth. Humanity has benefited greatly from the discoveries of the Scientific Revolution and the Age of Enlightenment in the 17th and 18th centuries. It is commonly believed that these advances in Western thought have caused a falling away from belief in God. That may be true, but not for the obvious reasons. It is not scientific knowledge in itself that has caused the decline in belief, but the self-sufficiency it has brought. On a material level, at least in advanced countries, one can live comfortably without God. At no other time in human history have so many individuals had the freedom to choose their own destinies, determine their own futures, and owe nothing to God.

The Church has survived the trend towards unbelief by continuing to be the place, in theory, where the asking of questions is encouraged. I remember a slogan from years ago, "Jesus came to take away your sins, not your mind." The walk of faith requires a degree of skepticism so that one has an informed faith, rather than a blind one. With faith, there is a strong element of rational understanding. Through inquiry and evaluation, one can find abundant evidence of God's existence. By keeping an open mind, the seeker can begin to perceive how God is mysteriously involved in the life of creation, as both its author and sustainer.

There are various reasons why people deny the existence of God. Sometimes a person will demand proof, or a sign of God's existence—an expression of non-belief which Jesus often encountered. A person may be angry with God, especially if he or she has experienced a personal tragedy. "How could a loving God allow this to happen?" That is a common question for which there is no easy answer. Alternatively, a person may reject God but believe in something else—a political ideology, for example, or a social cause.

For some people, faith comes as a gift from God. Being a person of faith does not always depend upon our own efforts. Being generous, God can fill a person with faith, in order to move them along on their journey. When faith is a gift, it takes away the desire to claim it as a possession. Unearned faith is another manifestation of God's outpouring of love.

The life of faith is built upon a close relationship with God who loves us and who, like a loving parent, wants the best for us. Although we pray that we may not be brought "to the time of trial," (Matthew 6:13) our faith is often being tested. Faith places demand on us: namely that we are to trust in God when times are tough. Faith has a dynamic, or even elastic, quality: it stretches us in ways that benefit us. As St. Paul writes, our "suffering produces endurance, and endurance produces character, and character produces hope." (Romans 5:3-4)

Finally, faith has the power to reveal God's world in ways that the eye without faith cannot see. With faith, one can see how God is present in the joys and sorrows of life. "God is our refuge and strength, a very present help in trouble." (Psalm 46:1) Therefore, faith is linked to wisdom, and to a true understanding of reality. It is the eye of faith which gives life to the soul. As Jesus says, "if your eye is healthy, your whole body will be full of light."
(Matthew 6:22)

CHAPTER 3

Prayer

Jesus told them ...to pray always and not to lose heart.

(Luke 18:1)

While questions about God's existence can be pursued at leisure, they tend to have a greater immediacy in times of crisis. Talking to God—also known as prayer—is often an involuntary response to an acute need. When a boy possessed of demons is brought before Jesus, the boy's father pleads, "I believe; help my unbelief!" (Mark 9:17-29) Even those who do not believe in God, or who have no faith, can catch themselves praying.

Ideally, the practice of prayer in the life of a believer should be well established. Although faith can inform our understanding regarding the existence of God and the nature of reality, its value is only realized when a believer acts upon it. The gift of faith has a practical purpose: it encourages the believer to sustain, through prayer, a meaningful relationship with God. Faith without prayer is like owning a valuable car but keeping it locked in the garage.

Whenever I lead a study course on prayer, I ask participants to say what they think prayer is. There are usually a variety of responses.

Here are some recent examples:

- Help, guidance, mercy—saying thank you;
- Being with God in silence. Deepening relationship;
- Interceding for friends, family, and for justice;
- Human's attempt to form a connection with the other unknown;
- Opening myself to God—listening to God's response;
- Struggle and silent contemplative listening;
- Being conscious of God's presence;
- Talking with God—not necessarily telling Him what I want.

All of these answers are linked by the common desire to make a connection with the living God—in other words, each person is directing his or her thoughts away from themselves and towards God. This is the essence of prayer—to seek engagement with the One who is. Prayer is essentially a form of communion and communication.

There is a large volume of literature dedicated to the subject of prayer, and there are many different ways of praying. One person may be more receptive to one kind of prayer than another. It is all a part of the richness of our faith that we can pray in different ways. However, there are times when it is essential that we pray together—Sunday worship, for example.

I mentioned earlier that prayer is a "practice." Like a muscle, prayer needs to be exercised. Without prayer, we can become spiritually flabby, dull, and uncomprehending. By contrast, the fruits of a disciplined prayer include flexibility, responsiveness, and increasing spiritual awareness. Over time, prayer changes us. The correlative question to "Who is God?" is "Who am I?" If it is true that relationships change us, then our relationship with God can change us more than any other.

The changes that take place within us through our relationship with God may develop into a calling to serve God. Those whom God calls are chosen for a reason, which is to follow God's will. However, what does it mean to follow God's will? It involves the alignment of one's own identity with that of God. Cardinal John Henry Newman wrote, "To live is to change, and to be perfect is to have changed often." In the cardinal's understanding, "perfection" does not consist of being without flaw, but of being willing to change for the sake of God.

The engine of change is love. All healthy relationships require love to sustain them, and the relationship with God is no different. The benefits of this loving relationship are exponential. A heart that is warmed by the love of God can be a source of warmth to others. In the same way that the love of a mother for her first child does not diminish with the coming of her second child, so the love of God expands into the life (and lives) beyond our own. Through prayer, we are learning to trust in God and to discover the ways in which God is connecting us to others.

Chapter 4

Discerning God's Will

Your way was in the sea, and your paths in the great waters,
But your footsteps were not known.

Psalm 77:19

A t the outset, it was apparent that the first followers of Jesus were less than perfect. They were given to intemperate outbursts (Peter), and vainglory (James and John); one, Judas, misunderstood and eventually betrayed Jesus. The disciples were intolerant of foreigners and scolded children and the disabled. They seem depressingly representative of the rest of us. Yet—and this is the point—God chose them. The disciples possessed gifts and talents and were equally possessed of flaws and imperfections. God chose them as diamonds in the rough, as works in progress, as the raw material from which the kingdom of heaven could be proclaimed and realized.

How could such imperfect recipients of God's message ever hope to succeed? Imagine God is calling you, and your first question is, "What is God's will for me?" You become frustrated because it isn't always clear what God wants you to do. The mistake is to think that, in wanting to do God's will, you must completely abandon your own. The truth is more nuanced than that.

In my experience, God doesn't always make his will clearly known. And even if we know fully what God wants us to do, God never entirely takes away our own will.

Instead of choosing between God's will and your own will, the challenge instead is to discern God's will and, as closely as possible, weave God's will and your own will together. However, as your will is imperfect, you cannot expect that all that you say and do will always be in accordance with God's will. Does this mean you should give up trying to discern God's will? On the contrary, the closer you get to God, the more clearly will you know how to act in accordance with his will.

It was God's will that the disciples would follow Jesus, but when the time came for them to exercise their own ministry, and spread the gospel, it became clear that they had different ideas about how to do this. The same is true for the Church today: there is one gospel but many voices.

Here is a piece of advice for those who wonder, amid the clamor of voices, what is God's will for them. Find a place of solitude and silence, free from distractions, and ask God to show you his will. Remember that there will always be an element of your own will hiding within your desire to serve God. The benefit of knowing this is that it relieves you of the pride of certainty. While you can act with good intentions, you can never boast that everything you do is what God wants.

CHAPTER 5

Called by God

A calling tugs at you and will not let you go until you
do something about it—ignore it, dismiss it, or respond to it.
Rev. Russell Levenson, from *Witness to Dignity*

As faith grows, so does the call to serve God in a particular way, or in a specific situation. You can be called upon to pray for another in need, or to visit someone who is housebound or in a hospital. You may be asked to lend a hand in church, either behind the scenes or in serving at the altar. Someone may ask you to give a witness to your faith, by asking you why you believe in Jesus. These are examples of prayer, ministry, and witness, through which the church is made visible in the world.

In his book *Meet Jesus*, Rev. John Twisleton gives an example of how a regular act of prayer led to a specific call:

> *A young man attended a church whose grounds were popular with vagrants. As he passed these people on his way to worship, Sunday by Sunday, they became part of his prayer in church. Eventually, he felt that Jesus was asking him to raise interest in organizing a regular lunch for them. The lunch came to involve not just the church members but many others in the community who had a concern for the poor[1].*

---

[1] J. Twisleton, *Meet Jesus* (Abingdon: Bible Reading Fellowship, 2011) p. 117

In the New Testament, there are many examples of callings, some prosaic and others life-changing. In the Acts of the Apostles, the Pharisee Saul is on his way to Damascus to arrest Christians, when he is knocked off his horse. (Acts 9) Saul hears the voice of Jesus for the first time. Saul has lost his sight, so the voice of Jesus claims the whole of his attention. Saul's blindness is symbolic of his failure to see God at work in the new Christian community.

Eventually, his sight is restored as his faith in Christ becomes a reality. Paul takes on the life of an apostle, proclaiming the gospel in the towns and cities of the Mediterranean and beyond. St. Paul composed many letters, rich in learning and theology, to the early Christian communities. At the end of his letter to the Church in Rome, we hear the greeting of Tertius, who wrote the letter by hand as it was being dictated by Paul. (Romans 16:22) The call of Tertius at that moment is to be a scribe to the apostle Paul.

As we read the gospels, we notice what kind of relationship Jesus has with the disciples: instructing, leading by example, healing, sometimes chiding, and always loving. The disciples continue the work which Jesus has begun. And, like Christ, they are vulnerable to ridicule and scorn. That they are willing to do this suggests that they were already possessed of a strong faith, one that convinced them to accept this new undertaking, even without a clear idea of where it would lead. The choice was a risky one. Did they ever doubt? What did they think they were getting themselves into?

In answering the call of God, there is always an element of uncertainty, of the unknown—there is no guarantee of how things will turn out. The only certainty is that God will be faithful to the one who answers God's call.

A personal anecdote may illustrate how a call is answered. My own call was to ordained ministry, although it took a long time for me to accept it. At first, it was something I resisted, thinking that there were better candidates than me for this role. I lacked confidence, and when I compared myself to the clergy who would visit the church, I did not see myself as one of them. However, the call did not go away, as I had hoped.

At the time, I belonged to a welcoming church that shared the love of God in its worship and fellowship. Following a friend's advice, I joined a Christian meditation group. Out of the practice of prayer and meditation, my faith grew deeper—I was hearing things anew in the gospel every Sunday, and my spiritual horizons were expanding. I was feeling overwhelmed by God's grace, of receiving more than I deserved—more than one person needed. How could I respond? I spoke to my parish priest, who encouraged me to explore my vocation. That was the start of the long process of discernment which would eventually lead to ordination.

The call had its origins in my deepening love for God and from a deep sense of gratitude for the gift of faith. From the time when, in my twenties, I started to attend church regularly again, up until the point where I offered myself for ordained ministry, faith had transformed my understanding of the world and of myself. Now I faced the biggest change and challenge of my life: to serve as a minister in God's church.

It isn't always clear, at first, what God is calling any of us to do. Only a very few will be called into ordained ministry, or to the monastic life. Even then, not all will be accepted. This is a surprise to many who think that they will automatically be sent to seminary because they believe God is calling them there. In fact, the church tests one's call and also discerns God's will for the one called.

The call of God is the expansion of the kingdom of heaven into the world around us. Those who experience God's call will enter a period of self-examination or self-reflection about life and relationships, and an evaluation of one's gifts. As mentioned before, it usually involves changes, both large and small. These changes will be driven by the love of God in Jesus Christ, whose own self-emptying love becomes the template for our response to God's call. It means that we give ourselves wholeheartedly, without condition, "taking the form of a slave" (Philippians 2:7) so that our wills may more perfectly conform to God's own will.

Giovanni Paolo Panini, *Saint Paul Preaching in Athens*, 1734,
pen and black and gray ink with gray wash, heightened with white gouache on tan
prepared paper, 716 1/2 in. x 10 7/8 in., Joseph F. McCrindle Collection, National Gallery
of Art, Washington D.C.

CHAPTER 6

Gifts of the Spirit

Our response can be made only when
the Holy Spirit gives his inspiration and strength.
(Vatican II - "Missions")

There is a famous passage in the first letter to the Corinthians, where the apostle Paul describes the Holy Spirit at work in the lives of the faithful.

> *To each is given the manifestation of the Spirit for the common good. To one is given through the Spirit the utterance of wisdom, and to another the utterance of knowledge according to the same Spirit, to another faith by the same Spirit, to another gifts of healing by the one Spirit, to another the working of miracles, to another prophecy, to another the discernment of spirits, to another various kinds of tongues, to another the interpretation of tongues.*
> *(1 Corinthians 12:7-10)*

These gifts are defined primarily as spiritual, and are given for a particular purpose. They are gifts that allow the divine life to be expressed through human activity. God's intention is that each gift forms part of a greater whole. In other words, each gift complements the other, and together, within the complete offering of a church, they combine to meet the needs of both church and community. In this way, the spiritual becomes the practical, and vice versa. There is a saying attributed to St. Teresa of Avila which elegantly expresses how this works.

Christ has no body but yours,
No hands, no feet on earth but yours,
Yours are the eyes with which He looks
Compassion on this world,
Yours are the feet with which He walks to do good,
Yours are the hands, with which He blesses all the world.

There is a danger for Christians in imagining the combining of this spiritual and practical world in terms of a Utopia. The kingdom of heaven is very different from the human idea of Utopia. For example, gifts are apportioned unequally; indeed many people have more gifts than they know what to do with, while others seem to have only a meager portion. The reality of gifts, calling, and spirituality is much more complicated than it first appears.

Possession of an abundance of gifts can be a mixed blessing. External factors—upbringing, surroundings, circumstance—often restrict, diminish, or delay the use of gifts. The Rev. George MacDonald observes,

> *Sometimes there might be a delay in carrying out a calling without that calling being frustrated. You think yours it is to help the poor? But is it for you to say when you are ready? Willingness is not everything...while cultivating your gift and waiting the call, you may be in active preparation for the work in the coming life for which God intended you when he made you.*
>
> *(from Weighed and Wanting)*

MacDonald places "calling" within the eschatological dimension of our lives. That is to say, in our calling, we are to look beyond the here and now and to eternity. As Pope Paul VI wrote,

> *For God has called man and still calls him, so that with his entire being, he might be joined to Him, in an endless sharing of a divine life beyond all corruption.*
>
> *(Gaudium et spes. 18)*

There is no obvious answer as to why gifts are given which remain unused. However, the call to serve God may involve the renouncing of a gift, which then serves as a kind of offering, or sacrifice. To illustrate this point, I know of a concert pianist who had a calling to devote her life to prayer. Her gifts offered her an alternative career as a professional musician. However, since her call to prayer was stronger than her call to music, she entered a convent and became a nun. Of course, there was a third way, involving a compromise between music and prayer. However, she had a specific call to pray within a monastic community, which superseded all other calls. Some think that those who join monasteries are running away from life but, as most religious will tell you, the opposite is true; the cloistered life can be as challenging and authentic as any lived outside. What motivated her was an overwhelming love for God, for whose sake she was willing to sacrifice her musical career.

For others, a call to serve may not at first be realized if one's gifts are offered but then declined or refused. For example, a church member felt a calling to train for the ministry. He spoke to his priest, who referred him to another priest for a six-month period of discernment. At the end of this time, the priests conferred and agreed that they would not recommend him to proceed further with his call to ministry. The person possessed many gifts, but the priests deemed that it would be better for all concerned if he found another way to fulfill his calling. In the end, with the continuing advice of his parish priest, the church member was encouraged to use his gifts in areas of non-ordained ministry.

Someone once said that "God doesn't call the equipped; God equips the called." But how exactly does God equip the called? Although some gifts are innate, others can be acquired from experience or learned through practice. My own experience is relevant here. As outlined earlier, in my late forties I decided to follow a call to ordained ministry. There were a number of reasons for not following this call: chief among these was my nervousness in front of groups of people, and the fact that I was hopeless at public speaking. There was an incident I remember vividly from that time when I worked for a bank. During a weekend conference, I was called upon to give a short, unscripted presentation. When the time came, I rose to speak but, as I looked out on the sea of faces, no words came from my mouth. I had completely frozen, and stood there until a colleague came up to rescue me. I had suffered a bad attack of stage fright.

It was an experience that should have served as a warning never to pursue a vocation that relies on public speaking! It was surely complete madness to have even considered pursuing my call any further. However, I stubbornly believed that God was calling me to the ministry. As luck (or grace) would have it, so did a number of people in the church, including my priest. The "equipping" eventually came at theological college when I shared my fear with the college principal, who would listen to me preach and then make constructive suggestions. With his patient encouragement, and with much prayer and practice, I began to develop the skills needed for preaching.

Finally, I believe that a good way to acquire spiritual gifts is simply to ask for them. Of course, God already knows what you need, but if you ask for the gifts you think are needful, God will supply you with what is necessary. It is worth bearing in mind that a willingness to serve God might be the only gift you have. You can approach service in the same way that a beggar approaches Jesus for help (Luke 18:35-43) That way, your poverty of spirit will be a blessing to yourself and to others.

CHAPTER 7

Servants of God

Whom shall I send, and who will go for us?

(Isaiah 6:8)

Is everyone called by God? The answer is yes, although every call from God should have its origin within the context of community life. Even a hermit must pray for the world, and for the community that nurtured and supported his or her call. At the other end of the scale, is volunteering to do the coffee hour at church really a calling? Arguably, yes—it is a calling with a small "c", but it is still a calling. It is an act of *service*, which lies at the heart of Christian life.

Whom does God call, why, and when? This book attempts to answer these questions with reference to the servants of God. In the second part, I will explore the lives of six Bible characters—Jacob, Moses, Judith, Samson, Samuel, and Mary—and consider why God called them and how they answered the call. Each has a different story to tell.

With Jacob, I was interested in how his upbringing affected his personality, and how he wrestled with unresolved childhood issues as an adult. I offer an original interpretation of a key event in Jacob's life from the book of Genesis.

In order to imagine Moses' experience of meeting God in person for the first time, I have drawn inspiration from the poem *Fire in the Earth* by David Whyte.

From the Apocrypha, I have taken the story of Judith, a soldier for God, who has a unique plan to deliver her nation from the hands of the Philistines. The success of Judith's mission depends upon a combination of daring and absolute faith.

Three of the characters chosen—Judith, Samson, and Samuel—were "Judges", who assumed judicial or military leadership of Israel against its enemies. Samson, who ruled as a judge for twenty years, is perhaps the best known. His relatively brief story is arguably the most exciting one in the Bible. Despite his obvious flaws, I make the case for Samson as a servant of God.

Samuel, once considered the author of the book of Judges, is a prophet, judge, and military leader combined. He obediently served God as leader, and just as obediently relinquished his leadership in favor of King Saul.

The final case study is Mary, the mother of Jesus. She is the only New Testament person to feature in this survey. When considering her call, I was inspired by the fresco of the Annunciation by Fra Angelico. Mary's "yes" to God's call was to change the course of human history. The most humble servant can have the greatest impact.

The third part of the book shifts the focus to four people I have known—two of whom have died and two who are still alive. These latter reflections will be more personal in nature. The intention is to provide modern examples to contrast with the better-known Bible stories.

God calls each one of us. The call does not depend on our worthiness or expertise. The kingdom of heaven is built by those who are faithful and willing, and who may be sinful or wounded, yet have a love for God and a desire to please him.

In the next chapter, I am providing a short guide for reading the Bible. The Bible is our main source for the lives of its characters. Can we rely upon it as a truthful witness? The Bible's claim to truth does not rest on our usual and reasonable expectation that truth comes from evidence presented, from which facts and motives are determined. By that measure, the Bible does not pass the test. The Bible is filled with facts, but also with myths and legends. Separating one from the other is problematic, since truth can be as well represented by myth as by facts, something the authors of the Bible understood well.

Reading the Bible is sometimes like being an explorer in a foreign land. Yet there is something unchangeable about human nature that continues to explain why the lives and stories of the people of the Bible remain relevant for the modern reader. In the chapters that follow, the reader will find a diverse cast of characters who, in their own way, have answered the call to love and have served God to the end.

CHAPTER 8

The Living Word

Your word is a lamp to my feet, and a light to my path.
(Psalm 119:105)

At his coronation in May 2023, King Charles III was presented with a specially bound edition of the Bible. The tradition of gifting a Bible to the new monarch dates from 1689, when William and Mary received a copy at their own coronation. The Bible is, as the seventeenth century Bishop Compton stated, "the most valuable thing that this world has to offer. Here is wisdom. This is the royal law. These are the lively oracles of God."

The Bible is identified as a book of value which, in the words of the Book of Common Prayer, is "written for our learning…to hear, read, mark, learn and inwardly digest." However, wherein lies the Bible's *chief* value? Is it the Word of God? Is it a work of history? Is it a manual for living a good life? Or is it to be enjoyed aesthetically, for the beauty of its wisdom and poetry? The Bible's appeal is multi-faceted. It is both one book and many books.

Essentially, the Bible is a collection of ancient writings that tell the *story* of a people and their relationship with God. Each book in the Bible explores this relationship through the lens of history, biography, prophecy, wisdom, poetry, law, or a combination of any of these. Taken as a whole, the Bible is a kind of *document*, or group of documents, which tell us something about the people—the Israelites, mostly—for whom they were written.

The Bible claims to be more than a document of record, however: its other name is Holy Scripture, which implies that the words and stories of the Bible are shaped and formed by the spirit of God. The Bible's impact has been both cultural and religious. The God who shaped and influenced the events of 2,000 to 3,000 years ago—the time period in which the Bible was written—is the same God who speaks to believers today, through his written word.

For thousands of years, the Bible was the only book that most people knew. Passages were read aloud in the synagogue or the temple. Rabbis and scribes would debate the finer points of the law, asking what God really intended to teach. The Bible defined a nation and provided a written and living framework for its flourishing.

In the early Christian Church, the letters of the apostles began to establish a new body of Holy Scripture. Then, the oral remembrances of Jesus were translated into the written gospels of Mark, Matthew, Luke, and John—allowing the words and stories of Jesus to be studied and followed by the burgeoning Christian communities. The Bible—whether as the Hebrew Bible alone or in conjunction with the New Testament—was the primary medium for community understanding, rules, and behaviors, and in particular for reminding the people of their obligations before God.

Reading the Bible presents an immense challenge. If you include the Apocrypha, the Bible comprises a total of 73 books. It separates into two sections: The first section is the Old Testament, or Hebrew Scriptures, while the second section is the New Testament, being the story of Jesus and his followers.

Where to begin? Open a page anywhere in the Bible (and many do) and you could find yourself reading about wisdom, genealogy, incest, decapitation, love poetry, or the end of the world. Perhaps the best place to begin is at the beginning, with the book of Genesis. God makes the world in six days and fills it with life. The world is a place of almost infinite diversity, from the smallest seed to "sea monsters and every living creature that moves." (Gen. 1:21) Human beings appear at the climax of God's creation. God made them in his own image, and gave them "dominion over the fish of the sea...

and over every creeping thing that creeps upon the earth." (Gen. 1:26) On the seventh day God rested: "God saw everything that he had made and, indeed, it was very good." (Gen. 1:31)

The Bible then traces the history of humankind, with a particular focus on God's chosen people, the Israelites. While it is possible to read the Bible from beginning to end, chronologically (although the events themselves are not always chronologically presented), the reader soon encounters interruptions to the flow of the narrative. In the book of Leviticus, for example, the precepts of the law are spelled out at great length. While essential to a student of the law, the details soon overwhelm the casual reader. Things slow down again in the book of Numbers, in the recording of genealogies. There are other books that seem to exist on their own terms, such as the book of the prophet Jonah, or the book of erotic love poetry known as the Song of Songs.

As an alternative to the book of Genesis, the first-time reader could start with the gospel of St. Luke or St. Mark, and then move on to reading the Letter to the Philippians.

Those who wish to know what a personal relationship with God is like could turn to the Psalms. Someone wanting to learn about Israel's kings could start with 1 Samuel (in this book there is a chapter on Samuel, prophet, and judge).

Another way of reading the Bible is to treat it as a collection of *biographies*. The Bible narrative is driven by the stories of its protagonists, such as Noah, the patriarchs Abraham, Isaac, and Jacob, the wise ruler Joseph, and Moses, Samuel, Saul, and David. They are the leaders of their people, and representatives of the struggle of Israel to establish its national identity and homeland. The Bible also tells the stories of Sarah, Rebekah, Rachel, Hannah, Judith, Ruth and Mary, and how each one played her part in the larger story of humankind's salvation. There is much human drama being played out in the pages of the Bible, which records both the successes and failures of a nation.

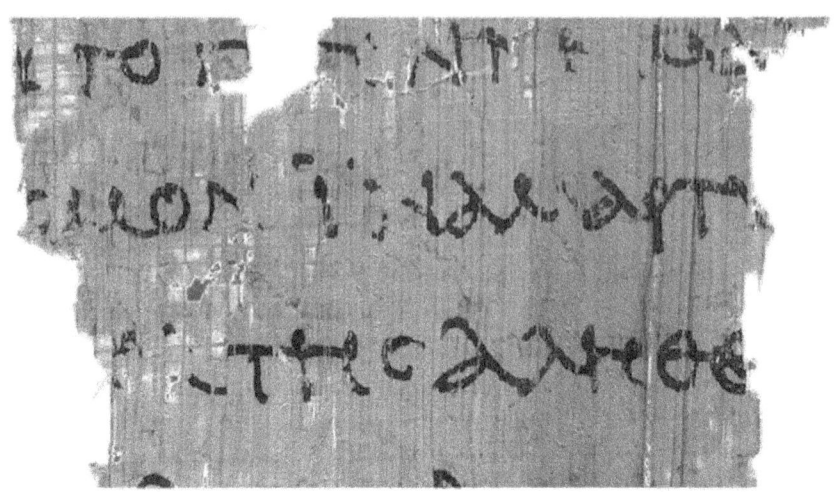

Most experts regard the fragments of *John Rylands Papyrus P52*, which contains part of the Gospel of John, as the oldest extant canonical Christian text.

John Rylands Papyrus P52, c. 125 - 140 A.D.,
fragment from a codex, 3 ¼ in. × 5 ½ in., John Rylands Library, Manchester, England.

The Bible has its own idea about how it should be read. It wants you to read it as the story of the *relationship* between God and humanity. *Relationship* lies at the heart of the Bible's message. Humanity's survival and flourishing depend upon a committed and faithful relationship with God. The original scheme of this relationship was *covenantal*, which later became codified into law. The law was holy because it came from God, and therefore the study of the law became a means of knowing God and of being in the right relationship with God. Later, with the coming of Christ, and the spread of the gospel by apostles such as Paul, the law was superseded by God's grace. That is not to say that the law was abolished. Rather, it was more that the personal and grace-filled nature of the God-human relationship became a central factor in the lives and fortunes of the early converts to Christianity.

Did the events in the Bible actually take place as described? This question arises as soon as one begins the first chapter of Genesis: "God made the world in six days and rested on the seventh." A person of faith is willing to believe that creation is the work of God. But did it all happen in six days? Evolution tells us otherwise. Here is the first challenge to the way we read the Bible—it cannot always be read as literal truth, or as a documentary narrative on the history of the world.

The idea of rigorous scholarship being applied to historical events was not foremost in the minds of the authors of the Bible. The creation story is an example of how truth and myth are woven together, not to falsify the story, but to emphasize a way of understanding God and the world. This understanding is intended to cohere with our own self-understanding. For example, when the first humans are driven out of the Garden of Eden because of their disobedience, we can relate that disobedience to our own behavior.

The blending of truth and myth actually reflects the way we tell stories about ourselves—to ourselves and to others. A story may be true, even though some of the details around the story have changed over time. Stories that depict acts of heroism and self-sacrifice extol the better parts of our nature. Myths, which are creative acts of memory, have the power to uplift and inspire us.

In the Bible, sorting fact from myth is nearly impossible. A good commentary can help, but there will be times when the reader must make a leap of faith. The phrase "leap of faith" can be misleading. In this context, it doesn't mean pretending something is true when you aren't sure it is. It means allowing yourself to become immersed in the Bible's narrative sweep—its stories, characters, landscape, lessons, beauty, poetry, cruelty, and profundity—without becoming bogged down in proving the veracity of its details. Unfortunately, with the passage of time, the Bible is the only resource we have for many of the characters and events it relates, especially where the Old Testament is concerned. Archaeology can sometimes throw light on the background of a person or place or event, but usually, we have no choice but to take the Bible at its word.

With the New Testament, the burden of truth is less of a problem. There are corroborating non-scriptural texts, such as the record of the first century Jewish historian Josephus, and of Roman commentators such as Lucian, who satirized Christians in the second century AD. Within the New Testament itself, the gospel accounts of Jesus' life and his challenge to the prevailing religious order are attested to and corroborated by the letters of the apostles. St. Paul's letters, in particular, are filled with religious and practical advice. In addition, we discover in Paul's letters the first examples of Christian theology. Paul, a Pharisee, explains how Christ fulfills the prophecies contained in the Hebrew Bible.

The letters of St. Paul, therefore, suggest another way to read the Bible: as *theology*. In the letter to the Romans, for example, Paul considers how, with the coming of Jesus, righteousness under the law has been superseded by the righteousness of faith. Paul brings his considerable intelligence to bear on various theological questions, in order to establish church doctrine and teaching.

Apart from Paul, another early theologian is the anonymous author of the Letter to the Hebrews. He shows how Jesus is our great high priest, who offers himself as a sacrifice for the sins of all. Jesus is both priest and victim. The letter also includes a roll call of those who have heard the call of God and answered in faith. (Hebrews 11)

Finally, it is possible to read the Bible purely as *literature*. Unmoored from the obligation to instruct and improve as God's holy word, the Bible stories can be enjoyed purely as stories or studies in human nature. This approach has its advantages, not least in freeing the reader from the traditional historical/critical interpretative method of study, which is the *modus operandi* of most Bible reading groups.

For example, the story of Jacob, who appears in the book of Genesis, provides a rich seam of material for the intrepid literary adventurer. His character lends itself to psychological analysis, and in the next chapter, I will dig beneath the surface of Jacob's life to reveal the inner tensions that drove him to seek reconciliation with himself and his brother Esau.

This book represents another way of reading, that is, *thematically*. I have taken the "call to love" as my theme, and have combined this theme with a biographical approach to understanding how the call to love is heard, embodied, and acted out.

Finally, a note on translations. There are many available, so it is important to choose the right one. Broadly speaking, translations fall into two camps, known as "functional equivalence" and "formal equivalence." The first attempts to translate the Bible into fluent and readable English, and uses expressions that do not always literally translate the original words. These translations have the advantage of appealing more to modern ears, but possess the disadvantage in that, paraphrasing what the translator thought the original authors were saying, one must rely on the judgment of the translator. Also, some translators may subtly alter the text in order to advance a theological or doctrinal position.

The second type of translation—formal equivalence—seeks to render the words of the Bible, which were originally in Hebrew or Greek, as closely as possible to their original meanings. This makes for a more accurate translation, and conveys the ancient mind better, although modern ears may find some passages challenging. In this book, I quote from the *New Revised Standard Version* (NRSV) and the *Revised New Jerusalem Bible* (RNJB). Students may like to compare the original *Jerusalem Bible* (functional-equivalence) first published in 1966, with its later, revised version RNJB (formal equivalence), published in 2019, to appreciate the differences between the two types of translation.

The Bible is a deep mine of wisdom, poetry and human drama, containing much to delight and stimulate both scholar and casual reader. Within its pages one can find advice for living and warnings for the future. As the evolving story of God and his people, the Bible reminds us that history is shaped by the partnership of God and his people, who are called to serve faithfully in God's world.

Part II
The Ancient Call

James J. Tissot, *Jacob Wrestleth with an Angel*, c. 1896-1902,
watercolor, 10 in. × 7 in., Jewish Museum, New York City

CHAPTER 9

Jacob

The Call to Reconcile

The same night Jacob got up and took his two wives, his two maids, and his eleven children, and crossed the ford of the Jabbok. He took them and sent them across the stream, and likewise, everything that he had. Jacob was left alone, and a man wrestled with him until daybreak.

(Genesis 32:22-24)

Alone beside the Jabbok River, Jacob wrestles with a mysterious figure. The encounter takes place at night, on the eve of a meeting between Jacob and his brother Esau. Jacob is facing death at the hands of Esau, whose birthright Jacob had taken from Esau many years before. Killing Jacob would restore the birthright to Esau, and make Esau the patriarch of Israel.

It is a moment of high narrative tension in the story of Jacob. Who is the man who wrestles with Jacob until dawn? Is he real, or a figment of Jacob's imagination? What are Esau's real intentions with regard to his brother? In this chapter, I will attempt to unravel the mystery of the encounter by the Jabbok River. I will explore the character of Jacob, especially in relation to Esau, and recount the key moments of his life. Finally, I will explain the psychological forces that drive Jacob, and how they culminate in the extraordinary struggle with the unidentified man.

Jacob's personality is complex. He is obedient, deceitful, calculating, resourceful, and always mindful of God's presence. His life is unpredictable and colorful, with many twists and turns. He survives the many challenges of his life through a combination of cunning and grace. God favors Jacob and affirms Jacob's call to serve as the leader of his people.

Jacob's parents were Isaac and Rebekah, and his twin brother was called Esau. Jacob's name is a play on words: the original meaning for *Ya'aqob* – "May God Protect"—is punned with *aqeb*, "heel," which is a reference to his birth. Esau is born first, and Jacob is born gripping his brother's heel. The two brothers could not have been more different. Esau "came out red, all his body like a hairy mantle." (Gen. 25:25) Jacob later describes himself as being "of smooth skin." (Gen. 27:11) They are also different in nature: Esau is a hunter, "a man of the field" (Gen. 25:27), whereas Jacob "was a quiet man, living in tents." (Gen. 25:27) We learn that Isaac, their father, "loved Esau, because he was fond of game", whereas Rebekah, their mother, "loved Jacob." (Gen. 25:29)

Jacob reciprocates his mother's love by staying at home and doing the cooking. Esau, meanwhile, enjoys the life of an outdoorsman. In contrast to his domesticated brother, Esau is a hunter of wild game. He is hairy and impulsive, almost a caricature, who upsets his mother and father by taking two local Hittite women as wives. (Gen. 26:34-35) As firstborn, Esau is his father Isaac's successor. According to tradition, he will receive his father's blessing—his birthright—and inherit the mantle of patriarch.

Esau's manly qualities are not allied to a sharp intelligence, however, and one day after hunting he returns home and carelessly trades his birthright for a bowl of stew. Esau is famished when he arrives home and notices that Jacob has been cooking. Esau demands a bowl of stew but Jacob will only let Esau have it in exchange for his birthright. Overcome by hunger, Esau agrees to the transaction not really thinking through the consequences of his action. Now everything has changed with Esau's foolish decision to trade his precious birthright. For Jacob, gaining the birthright was a first step: for it to become fully his own, he must now obtain his father's blessing. The elderly and blind Isaac will not willingly agree to bless the second-born son, so Rebekah devises a plan that will involve Jacob assuming the identity of his hairy brother Esau. Jacob will wear a goatskin to imitate the tactile and olfactory characteristics of his brother. (Gen. 27:6-29)

The deception is successful since Isaac smells and feels the goatskin worn by Jacob and believes that it is Esau. The old patriarch then blesses Jacob, thus completing the transference of the birthright from Esau to his younger brother. (Gen. 27:18-29) When Esau returns home and discovers the deception, he is enraged and threatens to kill Jacob. (Gen. 27:41-42) Fearing for Jacob's life, Rebekah sends him away to the distant town of Haran, to live with Jacob's uncle Laban, "until your brother's fury against you turns away." (Gen. 27:44)

After leaving home, Jacob travels alone to his uncle's land. At night, in the loneliness of the desert, he dreams of a ladder or ramp between heaven and earth "and the angels of God were ascending and descending on it." (Gen. 28:12) There the Lord appears to him saying, "Know that I am with you and will keep you wherever you go, and I will bring you back to this land; for I will not leave you until you have done what I promised you." (Gen. 28:15) These words become a guiding principle that governs the course of his life. When Jacob awakes from his dream he exclaims: "Surely the Lord is in this place – and I did not know it!" (Gen. 28:16)

Jacob's dream is significant because God confirms the blessing he has received from Isaac. The story of Jacob is also God's story. The story introduces a new theme: God favors the younger son to carry forward the patriarchal inheritance, a theme which later recurs with Joseph and David.

We follow Jacob on his flight north until he reaches the home of his uncle Laban. There he meets and falls in love with Rachel, Laban's youngest daughter. Jacob desires to marry her but, without possessions, he can only offer his labor to Laban in exchange for Rachel. Laban accepts, and for seven years Jacob works as a herder of Laban's flocks. At the end of this time, he rightly expects to receive Rachel as his bride, but on the wedding night, it is her elder sister Leah who comes veiled to the bridal bed. This trick enables Laban to negotiate a further seven years of free labor from Jacob. In return, Laban promises his daughter, Rachel, this time without any deception. In all, Jacob actually works twenty years for Laban (Gen. 31:41) and proves himself a useful shepherd, increasing the size of Laban's flocks many times over. (Gen. 30:30)

When the time comes for Jacob to leave his father-in-law, he contrives an elaborate scheme to acquire the best animals from Laban's flocks. (Gen. 30:35-43) When Laban discovers this final "trick" from Jacob, and learns that Jacob has left with wives and property, the older man sets off in pursuit. Laban takes with him a group of armed men and eventually catches up with Jacob. It seems that Jacob's deception will be his undoing. However, the night before, the Lord appeared in a dream to Laban, saying "Take heed that you speak to Jacob neither good nor bad." (Gen. 31:29) Laban also lacks the support of his daughters who take Jacob's side. By failing to pay Jacob his wages, Laban has, in the eyes of Leah and Rachel, "sold" them and "has been using up the money given for us." (Gen. 31:15)

In their final encounter, Jacob and Laban are reconciled, although in the exchange Laban has lost both daughters and a sizable number of sheep and cattle. The outcome marks a turning point in Jacob's life. In his dealings with Laban, he has emerged with a family of his own and considerable wealth in livestock. Before, he lived under the yoke of his father-in-law, but now he is head of a new "house" that carries his name. He has acquired status for himself, which allows him the freedom to decide his own future. However, this freedom is predicated on cooperation with God, who has delivered Jacob from the wrath of his uncle.

There is a favorable omen following the peacemaking with Laban. "Jacob went on his way and the angels met him." (Gen. 32:1) Jacob is now free to journey anywhere with his household, but where? Following the meeting with Laban, Jacob sends envoys to his brother Esau, with the message that he, Jacob, hopes to "find favor in your sight." (Gen. 32:5)

The messengers return with alarming news: "Esau...is coming to meet you, and four hundred men are with him." (Gen. 32:6) This number of men is consistent with a regiment of soldiers or a raiding party. Jacob and his new "house" are facing imminent oblivion at the hands of a vengeful brother. Jacob quickly devises a strategy that will ensure that not all of his "house" are wiped out. He divides his retinue into two companies. If "Esau comes to one company and destroys it, then the company that is left will escape." (Gen. 32:8) This action highlights the theme of division and the need for unity that characterizes Jacob's life. The scholar Robert Alter observes that:

A law of binary division runs through the whole Jacob story: twin brothers struggling over a blessing that cannot be halved, two sisters struggling over a husband's love, flocks divided into unicolored and particolored animals, Jacob's material blessing now divided into two camps.[1]

The primary division is located in the relationship between Jacob and Esau. Growing up together, the twins would have experienced typical sibling rivalries and the need for paternal approval. Isaac favored his more "masculine" son Esau over the more "feminine" Jacob. The sensitive Jacob would have been acutely aware that his father's favorite was Esau. His brother's "superiority", at least in his father's eyes, along with his masculinity and natural prowess, would have forced Jacob to "accommodate" his brother's natural exuberance at home, and one can surmise that living together would have been possible only if Jacob had had "coping strategies" with respect to his boisterous and child-like brother. The tension between these two brothers, each with their very different personalities, recalls Cain and Abel; however, the story of Jacob and Esau was to have an entirely different outcome.

To prepare for the encounter with his brother, Jacob offers up a prayer to God to "deliver" him.

Jacob said, "O God of my father Abraham and God of my father Isaac, O Lord who said to me, 'Return to your country and to your kindred, and I will do you good,' I am not worthy

of the least of all the steadfast love and all the faithfulness
that you have shown to your servant, for with only my staff I
crossed this Jordan; and now I have become two companies.
Deliver me, please, from the hand of my brother, from the
hand of Esau, for I am afraid of him; he may come and kill
us all, the mothers with the children. Yet you have said, 'I
will surely do you good, and make your offspring as the sand
of the sea, which cannot be counted because of their
number.'"

(Gen. 32:9-12)

It is the only extended prayer in the whole of Genesis, notable for its clear structure: address; self-abasement and description of current position; a call for deliverance; and a final "reminder" to God to keep his end of the bargain: "Yet you have said, 'I will surely do you good'." At the center of the prayer is the person of Esau, from whom Jacob seeks God's protection. What is notable is how differently Jacob reacts to the crisis, when compared to previous crises. After receiving Isaac's blessing, and when acquiring Laban's livestock, Jacob reacted by running away. Now he will stand and meet his brother, and trust in God. When the prayer is over, there is no further talk of escape.

But Jacob is still calculating and looking to influence the outcome of the meeting. With Esau approaching, Jacob concocts an additional strategy of appeasement. He makes Esau a peace offering—several in fact—that are exceedingly generous: a total of 550 animals in three stages. The Hebrew word for "appease" is *kpr*, usually rendered as "atone."[2] This suggests that there is more to the planned meeting than simply a desire to meet on peaceful terms. Jacob is, in the modern terminology, looking for "closure", not simply to draw a line under the past, but to redeem it. Jacob tells himself,

I will wipe the anger from his face
With the gift that goes ahead of my face
Afterwards, when I see his face

---

[2]*W. Brueggemann, Genesis. (Atlanta: John Knox, 1982), p.266*

Perhaps he will lift up my face!
The gift crossed over ahead of his face…

(Gen. 32:20-21)

In this literal translation by Everett Fox, the Hebrew word "face" appears five times.[3] When he says, "Perhaps he will lift up my face!" he is using an idiomatic Hebrew expression that denotes forgiveness. There is a link back to Cain: "The Lord said to Cain, "Why are you angry, and why has your countenance fallen?" (Gen. 4:6).[4]

The theme of the "face" is taken up by Ellen van Wolde, who notes that

> …*it looks as if the story of Cain and Abel is only about what the Jewish philosopher Levinas was to call "the face of the other". The criterion of action for a human being is not defined by his or her own autonomy but by the face of the other, which shows what is to be done and allowed to be done. That is why Cain's failure to look at Abel is so significant: he does not look into the face of the one who is his brother.[5]*

The similarities between Cain and Jacob are telling: both were jealous of their siblings and in their families, both were the least favored; because of their own actions, they were forced to leave home. Yet there is one important distinction: Cain commits the crime of murder. Initially, he shows no remorse for his action and no feeling for his brother. He is then marked by God for his sinful act and, as we shall see, Jacob too will be marked as a result of his encounter with the "man."

To return to our story, Jacob is preparing to meet Esau face-to-face. In the middle of the night, he crosses the ford at Jabbok with his wives, maids, and children, and everything else he has. The story continues…

---

[3]Everett Fox, *The Five Books of Moses*, (New York: Schocken Books, 1995) p. xi
[4]M.P. Korsak, *At The Start*, (New York: Doubleday, 1993), p.13
[5]E. Van Wolde, *Stories of the Beginning*, (London: SCM Press, 1996), p.83

Jacob was left alone; and a man wrestled with him until daybreak. When the man saw that he did not prevail against Jacob, he struck him on the hip socket; and Jacob's hip was put out of joint as he wrestled with him. Then he said, 'Let me go, for the day is breaking.' But Jacob said, 'I will not let you go, unless you bless me.' So he said to him, 'What is your name?' And he said, 'Jacob.' Then the man said, 'You shall no longer be called Jacob, but Israel, for you have striven with God and with humans, and have prevailed.' Then Jacob asked him, 'Please tell me your name.' But he said, 'Why is it that you ask my name?' And there he blessed him.

(Gen. 32:24-29)

This episode, which is highly unusual even by scriptural standards, invites multiple interpretations. On the surface it appears to be an encounter with a mysterious and unknown figure, but it will have profound life-changing ramifications for Jacob, his identity, and his relationship with his brother Esau.

Despite losing his inheritance, Esau has nevertheless prospered in the intervening years. Like Jacob, he has amassed significant material wealth, but in addition he commands a regiment of soldiers. Esau is a fighting man; the natural masculine tendencies in youth are now fully realized in adulthood. It is assumed that he has come to fulfill his earlier promise to avenge the wrong done to him all those years ago. (Gen. 27:41) Jacob, unarmed and vulnerable, faces his worst fear: that his peace offering will be spurned and that he and his family will be massacred.

Jacob wrestles with a man in the dark. (Gen. 32:25) The fact that the struggle occurs beside a river and the man cannot remain after daybreak might allude to river spirits or demons from folklore. However, the author of the story merely uses this as a literary device to suggest a supernatural encounter, not necessarily one of good against evil. The last time Jacob was alone in the desert at night, he dreamed of a ramp connecting heaven and earth. In this meeting, perhaps also a dream, he struggles with a man—*ish* in Hebrew—

who could be God, an angel, Esau or Jacob himself, or perhaps a combination of all of these.

In dreams our subconscious is free to engage with unresolved issues that are suppressed in our normal day-to-day existence. The largest unresolved issue in Jacob's life at that time was his relationship with Esau. There is guilt, (but not remorse), over his acquiring Isaac's blessing by deception. There is also the fact of their different natures—one traditionally masculine, the other feminine—that would have been associated in Jacob's mind at an early age with the notion of blessing and paternal acceptance. Jacob's father Isaac loved Esau the hunter more than the sensitive Jacob. Unable to compete with his brother, Jacob stayed at home under the feminine influence of his mother, devoting himself to cooking and domestic work. He buries the hurt of his father's rejection of him, and of his father's approval of the masculine elder brother.

Their imminent meeting has the effect of releasing this buried material from Jacob's subconscious. In her analysis of Hebrew terminology for man, van Wolde identifies that "man seen in relation to woman is called *ish*."[6] The struggle with the *ish* in Jacob's dream therefore involves a re-integration of these two natures, masculine and feminine, which culminates in a second and final blessing and a change of name and, by implication, identity. The father's blessing was therefore only half the story; Jacob needed to accept the "masculine" into his own identity in order to validate the blessing in his own mind. The fact that there is a struggle reflects the deep-seated resistance in Jacob to this integration. Jacob has wrestled throughout his life,

In his grabbing of Esau's heel as he emerges from the womb, in his striving with Esau for birthright and blessing…and in his multiple contending's with Laban. Now, in this culminating moment of his life story, the characterizing image of wrestling is made explicit and literal.[7]

---

[6]*Van Wolde, p. 139*
[7]*Alter, p.180*

Despite having already received his father's blessing, (Gen, 28:1) Jacob in his dream fights to receive a second blessing. "I will not let you go unless you bless me," he says to the mysterious figure. (Gen. 32:26) But *this* blessing is one he must give himself. There emerges now another theme relating to authority, and in particular to self-authorization. The mature Jacob must confront the fact that his status as patriarch was obtained by depriving Esau of his birthright. This ancient theme is in fact a modern one. Ambition and the desire to "move up the ladder" often involves advancement at the expense of others. For Jacob, it is to be worthy of leading his people, God's people. Jacob understands, whether consciously or subconsciously, that the inheritance he passes on must be undivided. It is not therefore an individual matter but one that is bound up with the history of his people. Not only is self-belief necessary, but in Jacob's case there also must be a necessary act of granting authority for himself, as a way of making the succession an effective one.

In recognition of this new authority, Jacob receives a new name, Israel. In uniting the divided natures of masculine and feminine in his dream struggle, Jacob is now worthy to assume the mantle for an entire nation. Because he prevails, Jacob has restored the unity of male and female in one person, but at a personal cost to himself, which takes the form of an injury.

At this stage, it is not apparent to Jacob exactly what has happened. Having been renamed Israel, there is then the following exchange between him and the "man" (who in his subconscious mind are the natures of himself and Esau): "Then Jacob asked him, 'Please tell me your name.' But he said, 'Why is it that you ask my name?'" (Gen. 32:29) The work of transformation is complete but Jacob in his misunderstanding asks the man for his name. "Why?" is the response, since the renaming has already taken place.

In a way, it does not matter that Jacob is unable to perceive the significance of this change, and in the future, the text will identify him at different times as both Israel and Jacob, perhaps in recognition of this fact. There is no question now that Jacob and the people of Israel are bound together in the quest to establish legitimacy.

There is a dietary prohibition that occurs at the end of Chapter 32, deriving from Jacob's wound.

The sun rose upon Jacob as he passed Penuel, limping because of his hip. Therefore, to this day, the Israelites do not eat the thigh muscle that is on the hip socket, because he struck Jacob on the hip socket at the thigh muscle.
(Gen. 32:31-32)

Most commentators believe this is a later addition to the text. Yet it is in keeping with the theme of "*change*—of place, parental line, name, alimentary rite."[8] The food taboo is to apply henceforth to the "Israelites", the first time this term is used. The author is deliberately linking Jacob/Israel to the future of the Hebrew people. The change of place is when Jacob calls the place Peniel—literally, "the face of God." (Gen. 32:31)

In his struggle with the "man", Jacob has sustained an injury to the hip. He emerges limping from the battle—the pain that comes from accepting one's own authority?—but claims a victory as one who has seen God "face-to-face." (Gen. 32:30) This extravagant statement is later put into proper perspective when he describes meeting Esau as "like seeing the face of God." (Gen. 33:10) In his dream, that is exactly what has happened. The work of reconciliation of identity and authority that was being wrestled with in his own subconscious is now fully operational at the conscious level. It may not become apparent to Jacob until he finally meets Esau on friendly terms. Even as he sees Esau approaching, he is still not sure if Esau comes in peace, so he divides his family into groupings, maids and children at the front and Rachel and Joseph at the rear.

He goes on ahead to greet Esau with a great display of deference, "bowing himself to the ground seven times." (Gen. 33:3) To everyone's surprise, "Esau ran to meet him, and embraced him, and

---

[8] *Barthes, p.136*

fell on his neck and kissed him, and they wept." (Gen. 33.4) Immediately the tension in the air has dissolved in a display of fraternal affection. Esau graciously refuses Jacob's peace offering of 550 animals, saying, "I have enough, my brother; keep what you have for yourself." But Jacob presses his brother to accept it, insisting

Please accept my gift that is brought to you, because God has dealt graciously with me, and because I have everything I want.
(Gen. 33:11)

Behind Jacob's deference and wish to make amends, he is quietly asserting his superiority.

Jacob says he has everything—on the surface, simply declaring that he doesn't need the flocks he is offering as a gift, but implicitly "outbidding" his brother, obliquely referring to the comprehensiveness of the blessing he received from their father.[9]

The two brothers go their separate ways. God's work of reconciliation has been done.

In conclusion, Jacob's life is one where chances are taken that count either for advantage or survival. His determination to prevail means he often has to struggle, or wrestle, to get his own way. Although he has to contend with both Esau and Laban, his greatest opponent is himself. His ambition to become the father of his people is impaired by his own vulnerability and fractured identity.

At his most helpless, he cries out to God for help, and it is God who saves him. Jacob's assertion of his right to his father's blessing is not without cost to himself and others. But the divisions that it created are, through his co-operation with the divine authority, eventually healed. In particular, Jacob subconsciously recognizes the need for a new identity that is appropriate to his new role. While he makes his plans and schemes, his subconscious delivers to him the opportunity to confront and wrestle with the divisions within

[9]Alter, p.186

himself. In overcoming these, he justifies not only God's faith in him, but he confirms his own desire to establish himself as the authentic leader of his people.

QUESTIONS FOR REFLECTION:

1. Sibling rivalry is a common feature in the book of Genesis. What do these relationships have to teach us about our relationship with God?
2. It takes a long time before Jacob becomes independent of his uncle Laban. Who in your church or community is not independent? Name the types of dependencies that we experience.
3. This chapter argues that Jacob had a divided nature, which needed to be reconciled. What needs to be reconciled or healed in your life and in the church today?
4. One the themes of the story is the importance of relating to one another "face-to-face." How can we encourage more face-to-face contact in our lives?

CHAPTER 10

Moses
The Call to Lead

An encounter with the living God—the God of Abraham, Isaac, and Jacob—is probably the last thing on Moses' mind as he guides his father-in-law's flock along the slopes of Mt. Horeb. Moses hears a voice speaking to him from a burning bush. As Moses slowly approaches the bush, the voice orders him to remove his sandals. The voice then says,

> I am the God of your father, the God of Abraham, the God of Isaac, and the God of Jacob…I have observed the misery of my people who are in Egypt; I have heard their cry…I have also seen how the Egyptians oppress them. So come, I will send you to Pharaoh to bring my people, the Israelites, out of Egypt.
>
> (Exodus 3:6,7, 9, 10)

Moses hides his face as he listens to God's words. After hearing God's plan, Moses is reluctant to commit himself. In the first instance, he doesn't understand why God would call him to take on such a monumental task. Unlike Samuel, who is counseled by the old priest Eli to say "yes", Moses weighs up God's ambition against his own, and decides that the job is beyond him.

"Who am I that I should go to Pharaoh, and bring the Israelites out of Egypt?" Moses asks. It is hard not to sympathize with Moses who, at the time, was happily married and living as a shepherd.

Moses thinks, not without reason, that the people will not accept his authority. He has a problem with speaking, being "slow of speech and slow of tongue." God goes to great lengths to affirm Moses in his calling, and promises Moses that "I will be with you." (Ex. 3:12)

This is the first of many conversations between God and Moses. In the book of Exodus, God lays out his plan and Moses finds excuses not to be a part of it. Eventually, however, Moses is won over. God's argument and reassurances are enough to persuade the reluctant shepherd to follow God's call. It is questionable, however, that argument alone would have convinced Moses to accept. Were there any other factors involved in Moses' decision?

It is probable that, in addition to hearing God's voice, Moses would have experienced an emotional and physical charge when meeting God for the first time. How far was Moses guided in his decision-making by what he was feeling? Unfortunately, the author of the story does not tell us. However, there is nothing to stop us from imagining what Moses felt like when he spoke with God that day.

Few writers have put themselves in Moses' sandals—or rather, his bare feet—in the way that the poet David Whyte has in his poem *Fire in the Earth*. The poem describes the visceral and spiritual reaction of Moses when he meets God. The poem begins,

> And we know, when Moses was told,
> in the way he was told,
> "Take off your shoes!" He grew pale from that simple
>
> reminder of fire in the dusty earth.
> He never recovered
> his complicated way of loving again
>
> and was free to love in the same way
> he felt the fire licking at his heels loved him.
> As if the lion earth could roar
>
> and take him in one movement.

Domenico Fetti, *Moses before the Burning Bush*, c. 1613 - 1614,
oil on canvas, 66 1/10 in. x 44 in., Kunsthistorisches Museum, Vienna

The line "he grew pale" immediately takes us into the inner realm of Moses' experience. "He…was free to love in the same way he felt the fire licking at his heels loved him" allows us to imagine a barefoot Moses feeling the fire rise up from the earth and flow into his body, like a flame of love engulfing and transforming him. This fire is God's spirit, making a holocaust of Moses' own "complicated way of loving" in order to call Moses into a new reality.

What the poet is depicting is a *religious* experience. In one sense, it is a pivotal moment in the life of the future leader of Israel. In another sense, it is a physical and spiritual eruption that touches and ignites every fiber of Moses' being. Indeed, it is difficult to believe that Moses' encounter with God would not have had a mystical element. The point is to emphasize how this unique experience will redefine Moses' own sense of self. As he is inflamed with the Spirit of God, Moses is being forged into the role to which God has called him.

God tells Moses to take off his sandals. This is what a servant does, as a way of showing respect before God. As Moses' bare feet touch the earth, it is a reminder of his origin, of being from the dust. (Genesis 2:7) It echoes the words from our funeral service: "Earth to earth, ashes to ashes, dust to dust." When Moses stands on holy ground, he apprehends his own mortality while feeling, at the same time, intensely alive.

Moses' experience eventually changes his self-understanding. On the one hand, his encounter with God will leave many things *unchanged*: Moses continues to doubt his abilities, and God's plans for him, and he questions God at length, not so much on why God is asking him, but *how* he, Moses, could possibly fulfill God's call. God says, to reassure him, "I will be with you." As God speaks to Moses from the burning bush, he intends Moses to understand that the "I Am" of God, will be joined to the "I am" of Moses.

With his feet on the ground, before the burning bush, Moses affirms his calling. He feels the power of the Spirit working within him, transforming not only his will but orienting his whole being toward a life of serving God.

God has chosen him for a reason. Moses has strengths in the areas God needs—faithfulness, intelligence, persistence, and, perhaps most importantly, righteousness. Through righteousness, Moses can know and fulfill God's will. God's reassuring words to Moses—"I will be with you"—help to convince Moses to place his trust in God's providence for him. At the same time, these words indicate God's trust in Moses. The work of liberation depends on the sum of the two: "I AM" will become "WE ARE."

QUESTIONS FOR REFLECTION:

1. Have you ever stood on holy ground, or found yourself in a 'thin place", where the barrier between God and us is almost unnoticeable?
2. In your own words, how would you interpret the line "he…was free to love in the same way he felt the fire licking at his heels loved him?"
3. Is there a connection or compatibility between faith and poetry? How does poetry expand our understanding of faith?
4. Is everyone called by God for service? Are bushes burning everywhere, but we miss the blazing?

CHAPTER 11

Samuel

The Call to Obey

In the hour before dawn, a young boy named Samuel is fast asleep in the temple. An oil lamp beside the Ark of the Covenant burns steadily, bathing the walls and ceiling of the temple in its soft light. In another room, Eli, the old priest who guards the temple, is also sleeping. Suddenly, a voice is heard within. "Samuel! Samuel!" The young boy rouses himself from sleep, and runs over to Eli, saying, "Here I am!" The old priest is perplexed by Samuel's statement and bids him to go back to sleep. Once more Samuel hears his name being called, and again he runs to Eli, who now assures the boy that he did not call him. When it happens a third time, Eli perceives that it is the Lord who is calling Samuel. Eli counsels the boy to answer, "Speak, Lord, for your servant is listening." Samuel does as Eli says, and the Lord appears before Samuel and speaks to him. (1 Samuel 3:1-10)

The Calling of Samuel is a well-known story. It is notable for several reasons: first, Samuel does not know that it is God who is calling him. God calls more than once before Samuel responds directly. Second, it is only through the intervention and counsel of a third party—the old priest Eli—that Samuel is directed to answer. Third, God calls Samuel in the temple, where Samuel serves and where God is present. God is calling Samuel to be the religious leader of his people.

The story of the prophet Samuel is found in the books 1 & 2 Samuel. Although these books carry the prophet's name, they are perhaps better known as the histories of the kings Saul and David. However, as the books are named after the prophet and not the kings, we can assume that Samuel's role in Israel's history is no less important than those of his illustrious successors.

God's call to Samuel comes prior to a calamitous military engagement between Israel and the Philistines when Israel's armies are defeated. Most disastrously of all, the ark of the covenant is taken by the Philistines as war booty. God perceives the need for strong, moral leadership, and to save Israel from further humiliation he has chosen Samuel to be its leader.

Samuel is a young boy when he is chosen by God, but he has the necessary inner qualities of faith, obedience, and steadfastness to carry out the role for which God has called him. At that time, the situation in Israel was dire, brought on by the corrupt behavior of Eli's two sons, the priests Hophni and Phinehas, who assumed that they would lead Israel following the death of their father. The sons of Eli have been diverting food offerings intended for the Lord to themselves, and have solicited sexual favors from the women serving at the entrance to the tent of meeting.

When God calls Samuel, it is to tell him that, in restoring Israel, the house of Eli will be destroyed, and Eli's sons killed. Samuel's first task is to convey this news to the old priest. At first, Samuel is reluctant to say anything that might upset Eli. To understand why, we need to revisit the events of Samuel's early life.

Samuel was the son of Elkanah and Hannah. Elkanah had two wives, but only Hannah was childless. Scripture explains that "the Lord had closed her womb." (1 Samuel 1:5) In those days, being childless was a source of shame, and Hannah grieved her barrenness. To make matters worse, she had to put up with the mocking of Elkanah's other wife, Peninnah. In despair, Hannah went into the temple at Shiloh and prayed to the Lord,

Carl Schuler, *Samuel Taught By Eli (1 Samuel 3, 1-19)*, c. 1850,
copperplate engraving after a painting (1780) by John Singleton Copley
(American painter, 1738 - 1815)

O Lord of hosts, if only you will look on the misery of your servant, and remember me, and not forget your servant, but will give to your servant a male child, then I will set him before you as a Nazirite until the day of his death.

(1 Samuel 1:11)

God heard her prayer, and Hannah conceived and bore a son, whom she named Samuel, meaning "God is his name." God's favor transformed Hannah's sorrow and humiliation into joy. She showed her gratitude by keeping her promise to God and gave her son—her firstborn—as an offering to the Lord. When Samuel was weaned, Hannah took him up to Shiloh and left him in the temple with Eli. Hannah prays again, in a famous song that begins, "My heart exults in the Lord; my strength is exalted in my God." (1 Samuel 2:1)

One can imagine that her joy was tempered with sorrow. The separation of mother and child would also have been distressing to both Hannah and Samuel. How did this experience affect Samuel? We can only guess, since the author of Scripture wants the reader to understand that it is loyalty and obedience, and not emotion that defines the righteous relationship with God. Throughout his life, where God is concerned, Samuel was to follow his mother's example of obedience.

God continued to bless Hannah after she returned home without Samuel. It is notable that, in Scripture, at any rate, the futures of mother and son are juxtaposed.

And the Lord took note of Hannah; she conceived and bore three sons and two daughters. And the boy Samuel grew up in the presence of the Lord.

(1 Samuel 2:21)

The Jewish historian Josephus believed that Samuel was twelve years old when he was called by God. At that age, a Jewish boy became "a son of the law", and henceforward would take full responsibility for his actions, especially with regard to following the precepts of the law. When God commands Samuel to tell Eli about the impending downfall of the house of Eli, Samuel is facing his first test of obedience. Understandably, Samuel is reluctant to pass on this prophecy to Eli. The news will be crushing for the old priest to hear. Since Samuel was left in Eli's care by Hannah, one can imagine that a close bond has grown between the priest and the boy. Perhaps the reason for Samuel's hesitance is due to his consideration of the old priest's feelings. In the end, Eli insists on hearing the news, knowing full well that God's judgment rests upon him. In his wisdom, the old priest is also affirming Samuel's call. After hearing Samuel's prophecy, Eli is resigned to his fate: "It is the Lord; let him do what seems good to him." (1 Samuel 3:18)

Following the deaths of Eli and his sons, the people do not immediately turn away from their worship of false idols. There is some consolation for Israel in the unexpected return of the ark of the covenant, which had proved more of a curse than a blessing for the Philistines. (They had experienced an epidemic of tumors).

The drift of Israel into idolatry meant that they needed someone who would provide strong moral and military leadership to pull them back. That someone was Samuel.

As an adult, Samuel assumes full responsibility for the leadership of Israel. His new role of Judge is a combination of leader and prophet. The memory of defeat at the hands of the Philistines still hangs heavy over the people. Samuel exhorts them to change their ways and trust in the Lord. He tells them,

> *If you are returning to the Lord with all your heart, then put away the foreign gods from among you. Direct your heart to the Lord, and serve him only, and he will deliver you out of the hand of the Philistines.*
>
> *(1 Samuel 7:3)*

The Philistines have assembled once more to attack Israel. Samuel offers a burnt offering and then calls out to the Lord "for Israel". In answer, "The Lord thundered with a mighty voice against the Philistines and threw them into confusion." (1 Samuel 7:10) The Philistines are routed in battle, and Israel regains the land it had lost. God's choice of Samuel as both prophet and leader has been vindicated. This represents the high point in the fortunes of Samuel. Yet the situation will soon change, and Samuel will step down to make way for the kings of Israel.

Ironically, Samuel's fault was the same as Eli's: both were poor parents, who were ineffective in applying the necessary discipline in their sons' upbringings. Samuel's sons neither honored nor feared the Lord. They "did not follow in his ways, but turned aside after gain; they took bribes and perverted justice." (1 Samuel 8:3) The elders of the people therefore met with Samuel to express their dissatisfaction and call for a king to govern them, "like other nations." Samuel is displeased and turns to the Lord for guidance. God's response surprises Samuel.

> *Listen to the voice of the people in all that they say to you; for they have not rejected you, but they have rejected me from being king over them…You shall solemnly warn them, and show them the ways of the king who shall reign over them.*
>
> *(1 Samuel 8:7-9)*

Samuel tries in vain to convince the people of the folly of their wanting a king, who will raise taxes and lord it over them. One suspects that, despite God's reassurances, Samuel feels the people's demand for a king is a judgment of his own sons and leadership. Samuel takes everything to God in prayer. God answers Samuel as before: "Listen to their voice and set a king over them." (1 Samuel 8:22) Although Samuel is reluctant, he obeys God's word. He will search for a king to lead the people. Eventually, he finds Saul and anoints him as the first King of Israel.

Saul will later be succeeded by David as king, whom Samuel will also anoint. As the story begins to focus more on Saul and David, Samuel's prophetic role increases, particularly as a critic of King Saul. The reader's attention is increasingly drawn to the rivalry between the kings, while the absence of psychological complexity in Samuel's character becomes noticeable. He is a trustworthy and obedient servant, who tirelessly prophesies for the Lord, never putting a foot wrong. Indeed, all of his prophecies come true. His claim to have been an honest, righteous, and upright ruler of the people is met without dissent. (1 Samuel 12:1-5) But Saul and David, who follow him in the story, have more interesting personalities and adventures.

Samuel judges Israel for over forty years. His death is mentioned in passing at the beginning of chapter 25. It reads simply,

Now Samuel died; and all Israel assembled and mourned for him. They buried him at his home in Ramah
(1 Samuel 25:1)

What can we learn from the life of Samuel? First, that he was an answer to prayer, for his mother Hannah, and later for the people of Israel. He answered the call of God in accepting the role of prophet and judge. He died as the last representative of the judges who had ruled Israel for centuries. If, as St. Paul declares, the gift of prophecy is given in proportion to faith, (Romans 12:6) then Samuel's faith was like an overflowing cup, and his prophecy a reliable beacon of truth at a time when Israel needed it most.

Samuel followed God's will throughout his life, even stepping down as leader so that another—a king—could take his place. It is a sign of his humility that he could anoint the new King Saul and then take the time to write down the "rights and duties of kingship" in a book. (1 Samuel 10:25) The transition of power from Samuel to Saul is also a rare scriptural example of democracy in action, where the will of the people for a king to govern them is granted.

Samuel had the conviction and courage to challenge the people on their worship of false idols. A prophet's voice is not always welcome, especially by those who have grown used to following their own ways. Yet God speaks through the prophets, in order to bring the people to their senses. Along with the Law, the Prophets play an essential role in guiding the nation of Israel in the way of righteousness, and in advocating for the life-giving relationship with the one true God.

Inevitably, Samuel's own importance as a judge is overshadowed by the rivalry between Saul and David. The Hebrew scholar Robert Alter names his translation of 1 and 2 Samuel *The David Story*. It is interesting to compare Samuel and David, two key persons in the history of Israel, whose personalities and lives were very different. Both were called at a young age, and both had a close relationship with God. David's honored successor will be Jesus. Yet Jesus' own character resembles Samuel's more than David's. The roles of prophet and leader, which were combined in Samuel, are re-established in Jesus. Yet Jesus is our King, in the line of David, who will rule in our hearts as the savior, not only of Israel but of the whole world.

The saying, "Cometh the man, cometh the hour," is true for Samuel. Israel needed a righteous prophet and judge like Samuel to lead them after the first disastrous war with the Philistines. Through Samuel's leadership, Israel's fortunes were restored and the people learned the importance of faithfulness to God.

They saw in Samuel a true spiritual leader, who was governed not by self-interest but by a sense of duty and service to God. In his farewell address (1 Samuel 12), Samuel reminds the people that his righteousness has been to their benefit. He has not exploited his position for personal gain but ascribes to the Lord the credit for their deliverance from oppression. Compared to David, Samuel may appear stiff and colorless, yet there are times when such people make the best leaders. If Samuel comes across as lacking emotional depth—which may well be the author's intention—that should not cause us to underestimate his importance as one of the saviors of Israel.

Anyone who thinks that they may have a call to serve God will sooner or later encounter Samuel. When, as a boy, he is called by God in the temple, Samuel did not know that it was the Lord who was calling him. The words given to Samuel by the old priest Eli to say—"Speak, Lord, for your servant is listening"—aptly convey the lively response of those called by God. A prophet, called to speak the word of God, must listen first to what God is saying.

QUESTIONS FOR REFLECTION:

1. Eli perceives that God is calling Samuel. Have you ever felt that God was calling someone you know, who was unaware that God was calling them?
2. As she promised, Hannah gives her son Samuel to God. Have you ever prayed to God and promised to do something in return?
3. Samuel says to God, "Speak, Lord, for your servant is listening," How do we listen to God? What is God saying to you?
4. Why are the qualities of obedience and humility important in the life of a servant of God? Can you name some other qualities?

CHAPTER 12

Judith

The Call to Act

The Apocrypha is a collection of Hebrew religious texts which range in date from 300 BC to the second century AD. For various reasons, mainly to do with questions of scriptural authority, the books of the Apocrypha were excluded from the official canon of Scripture. If they appear in the Bible at all, they are usually placed in a separate section, to denote their non-canonical status. However, as Martin Luther observed, "These are books that, though not esteemed like the Holy Scriptures, are still both useful and good to read."

The Book of Judith, which is included in the Apocrypha, is a story of a pious Jewish widow called by God to save the Israelites from annihilation at the hands of their enemies. As the people of Israel are encircled and laid siege by the army of the Assyrians, Judith steps forward with a plan to save her people: she goes into the camp of the enemy and kills its leader.

Judith's name means "the Jewess", and she conforms to a type of "savior" of her people: one who has courage and a strong faith, who can think clearly and exercise decisive leadership. Whether or not Judith really existed is impossible to verify. Her story blends history and myth into a gripping account of one woman's mission to deliver Israel from her enemies. The story is distinctive for two reasons:

first, the one who assumes the savior role is a woman, and second, her plan and its execution are unique in Scripture.

She was a favorite subject for artists, especially during the Renaissance. Caravaggio, Fontana, Allori, and Galizia all painted pictures featuring Judith. Perhaps the one who captures her best is the Italian artist Artemisia Gentileschi, who painted at least four canvasses of Judith. They usually depict the murder (or immediate post-murder), of the Assyrian military commander Holofernes. In one particularly graphic version, Judith draws a sword across the neck of the Assyrian commander, causing blood to spurt from his severed artery. Judith kills emphatically and without emotion, while Holofernes realizes too late that he is being murdered.

The Book of Judith opens with a description of the Assyrian King Nebuchadnezzar's attempts to gain allies in a military adventure. When this fails, the King declares war on his neighbors and begins a campaign to defeat his opponents and pillage their land. The king owes his success in battle to the skillful leadership of his military commander Holofernes. However, there is one nation that remains unconquered: the Israelites. When asked to surrender, they refuse. Holed out in their mountain fort of Bethulia, facing the powerful and all-conquering Assyrian army, it seems only a matter of time before the Israelites too, will succumb.

It's a familiar tale given a new twist, in that the one who saves the nation from almost certain destruction is a woman. Scholars have remarked that Judith represents an idealized version of Jewish womanhood. She is a widow: her husband Manasseh died and left his considerable estate to her, which allows her to live independently. She has mourned her husband's death for three years and four months, wearing "sackcloth next to the skin and dressed in widow's weeds." (Judith 8:5 RNJB) Judith is a devout woman, of whom no one speaks ill, and who "feared God with great devotion." (Judith 8:8)

She was beautiful to behold, a factor that would be crucial in her plan to defeat the Assyrians.

Artemisia Gentileschi, *Judith Beheading Holofernes*, c. 1614 - 1620,
oil on canvas, 78 3/10 in x 63 9/10 in, Uffizi Gallery, Florence, Italy

Interestingly, Judith does not appear in the book until halfway through. The first seven chapters are given over to describing the political and military background of the story. We meet the main players: King Nebuchadnezzar, his commander Holofernes, the Gentile prophet Achior, who tries to warn Holofernes against waging war, and Uzziah, the Jewish leader. On one level, the Book of Judith is a story about war and the imperial ambitions of King Nebuchadnezzar. The King's armies, under Holofernes' command, crush all opposition they meet, so that "dread and fear fell upon all." (Judith 2:28)

With the Israelites, Holofernes adopts a different strategy: to avoid unnecessary casualties when attacking uphill, he lays siege to the town and cuts off their water supply. This proves effective, insofar as the leaders of the Israelites are brought to the brink of surrender. The situation appears hopeless.

Uzziah, the Israelite leader, who sees the suffering of his people, decides that, if God does not come to their aid within five days, they will surrender. When Judith hears about the plan of Uzziah and the elders, she summons them to her tent. When they arrive, she castigates them for putting "God to the test." (Judith 8:12) She tells them,

> *You cannot plumb the depths of the human heart or understand the workings of the human mind; how do you expect to search out God, who made all these things, and find out his mind or comprehend his thought? No, my brothers, do not anger the Lord our God. For if he does not choose to help us within these five days, he has power to protect us within any time he pleases, or even to destroy us in the presence of our enemies. Do not try to bind the purposes of the Lord our God; for God is not like a human being, to be threatened, or like a mere mortal, to be won over by pleading. Therefore, while we wait for his deliverance, let us call upon him to help us, and he will hear our voice, if it pleases him.*
>
> *(Judith 8:14-17)*

In reply, Uzziah speaks of Judith's "true heart" and "wisdom." He exhorts her to pray for rain, so that their cisterns may be filled. But Judith wants God to assist in a more radical way.

She conceives an audacious plan to defeat the Assyrians: Judith and her maid will make their way to the Assyrian camp, gain the trust of the Assyrians, and kill their military leader. Because she does not trust them, Judith conceals details of the plan from Uzziah and the others, who nonetheless give their blessing. The plan is also hidden from the reader, although all will soon be revealed. At this point in the story, the focus is now resolutely on Judith, while Judith's focus is resolutely on God.

Before she acts, Judith prostrates herself before God and, in a lengthy and passionate prayer, calls on God to aid her deception. She pleads,

> *Make my deceitful words bring wound and bruise on those who have planned cruel things against your covenant, and against your sacred house, and against Mount Zion, and against the house your children possess.*
>
> *(Judith 9:13)*

What follows is a beautiful passage that details the preparation for her mission. It is made powerful by the emotion that is concealed below the surface of this simple description of a woman getting dressed.

> *Judith got up from the floor, summoned her maid, and went down into the rooms which she used on Sabbath days and festivals. There she removed the sackcloth she was wearing and, taking off her widow's dress, she washed all over, anointed herself plentifully with perfumes, dressed her hair, wrapped a turban round it and put on the robe of joy she used to wear when her husband Manasseh was alive. She put sandals on her feet, put on her necklaces, bracelets, rings, earrings and all her jewelry, and made herself beautiful enough to beguile the eye of any man who saw her. Then she handed her maid a skin of wine and a flask of oil,*

filled a bag with barley girdle-cakes, cakes of dried fruit and pure loaves, and wrapping all these provisions up gave them to her as well.

(Judith 10:3-5 RNJB)

There is a meditative quality to her preparation. One can imagine Judith, with each action, recalling how her beauty pleased her husband and how she once loved the luxury and ritual of adorning herself with jewelry and perfumes. She had not made herself up in this way since her husband's death. As she picks up each item in turn, how can she not now remember his love for her and her love for him? And now she will do something new for the love of him, to honor his memory, and to save her people from destruction.

As she gazes at her reflection in the mirror, one can also imagine that as Judith is admiring her own beauty, she is contemplating the violence she will visit upon Holofernes. However, her action will be preceded by another violence—violence to herself, to her feelings, as she feels the tide of emotion well up as she remembers her late husband. For her mission to be successful, she will need to suppress these feelings and gain mastery over her emotions.

The exterior transformation of the beautiful Judith is complemented by a very different interior transformation. The devout woman, so admired for her piety, beauty, and wisdom, must transform herself into a murderer. She must lie like someone who is practiced in lying. She must deceive as someone who is used to deceiving. She must gain the trust of her enemies and conceal her true intention, without arousing any suspicion. In a sense, she must become the opposite of who she is.

Judith's call is an unusual one—to fulfill the will of God, she must break God's commandments. But what alternatives remain for the Israelites who are besieged in their mountain top retreat? They face an efficient and ruthless fighting force under the skilled command of Holofernes. Were the Israelites to break out and attack

now, they would almost certainly be defeated. As it stands, they have no reasonable expectation of escaping annihilation.

So strong is her confidence in God, Judith prays for the seemingly impossible: for Israel to be delivered from her enemies. Judith realizes that action is needed on the ground before God will grant assistance. Judith's faith is reflected in these words to the Jewish leader Uzziah:

In spite of everything, let us give thanks to the Lord our God, who is putting us to the test as he did our ancestors.
(Judith 8:25)

Judith trusts God to fulfill her petitions. In her exhortation to the leaders, it is telling that Judith quotes the name of Jacob, who survived and prospered through a combination of cunning, ambition and God's help. Like Jacob, Judith prays to God for salvation. And, like Jacob, she has conceived a plan: to deal a mortal blow to the Assyrian force.

Her beauty and manner beguile the Assyrians when she meets them. They bring her in to the camp, and discover that her beauty is matched only by her eloquence in speech. When introduced to Holofernes, she flatters to deceive by saying "I will say nothing false to my lord this night," (Judith 11:5) and then proceeds to lie in every detail of her speech to him, except perhaps, when she says, "my lord will not fail to achieve his purposes," which can be taken as meaning that Holofernes will not fail, but also, in Judith's secret thought, that God will not fail.

Any initial suspicion that she may have aroused is dampened by her dignified behavior within the camp. She and her maid spend three days there, mainly keeping to themselves inside the tent provided for them. Each evening, Judith leaves for the valley of Bethulia, to bathe in the spring and pray to God "to direct her way for the triumph of his people." (Judith 12:8) On the fourth day, Holofernes holds a banquet for his personal staff, and invites Judith to attend. It turns out that Holofernes also has a plan. He says,

It would be a disgrace if we let such a woman go without having intercourse with her. If we do not seduce her,

[literally, 'enjoy her company'] she will laugh at us.
(Judith 12:12)

When invited to the banquet, Judith complies, saying, "whatever pleases him I will do." (Judith 12:14) Judith's maid places lambskins on the floor before Holofernes, and when Judith enters, she lies on the lambskins, arousing Holofernes with her charms. Although Holofernes is smitten by his ravishing guest, he doesn't make a move on her; instead, he imbibes an excess of alcohol, and passes out drunk in his tent.

Everyone had too much to drink that night, and all retired to their respective beds. Everyone, that is, except Judith and her maid. Judith directs her maid to stand guard at the tent's entrance, while Judith stands beside Holofernes' bed and surveys the sleeping body of the Assyrian commander. She prays to God—"O Lord God of all might" (Judith 13:4)—to look at the work of her hands as she delivers Israel from its enemy. The story continues,

> *Judith took down his sword that hung by the bed, took hold of the hair of his head, and said, 'Give me strength today, O Lord God of Israel!' Then she struck his neck twice with all her might, and cut off his head. Next she rolled his body off the bed and pulled down the canopy from the posts. Soon afterward she went out and gave Holofernes' head to her maid, who placed it in her food bag. Then the two of them went out together.*
> *(Judith 13:6-10)*

When Judith and her maid arrive back at Bethulia, she astonishes the people with her prize. As she pulls the bloody head of Holofernes out of the food bag, holding it up for all to see, she says, "The Lord has struck him down by the hand of a woman." (Judith 13:15) In response the people "bowed down and worshipped God." (Judith 13:17)

Soon after, Judith follows up her brave mission into enemy territory by assuming control over the Israelite army. She commands them to attack, predicting with total accuracy the panic that will spread among the Assyrians, once they find their leader dead. The Israelite army triumph in battle, laying waste the Assyrian army and slaughtering them in great numbers. The story concludes with Judith's song of praise to God, (which includes a generous acknowledgement of her own saving role). Because of her actions, Israel enjoys a long period of peace. Judith's maid is granted manumission, while Judith herself lives to the age of one hundred and five.

This account of the victory of Israel over its enemies exalts Judith as the pious and yet resourceful model of Jewish womanhood. When all seems lost for the nation, she conceives an audacious plan to save it. She is like a chess player who has lost material and faces defeat, yet at the last minute finds a way to swindle an improbable victory over her opponent.

The story also emphasizes God's role in inspiring and fulfilling Judith's plan. Judith is only able to carry out her plan because she is a person of prayer. She allies her bravery to God's strength, believing that only with God's help can her plan have any hope of success. Although she lives in a patriarchal society, in this case the patriarchs have failed. God therefore empowers Judith to save the nation, using those gifts which are not usually considered weapons of war: her beauty and holiness, which soften the hearts of her enemies and allow her to destroy them.

Judith appears a paragon of moral virtue, especially in displaying the virtue of courage. Yet her actions contain a paradox, in that she fulfills her moral and civic duties by behaving in an immoral manner, using deception and even committing murder. She is interesting from a psychological point of view, and the closer we get to her, the more challenging she appears. And since the story is about God as much as Judith, and about the close relationship between the two, the actions of Judith ask questions about our understanding of God, and how far God will go to fulfill his plan.

One answer to this paradox is that Judith becomes a soldier of the Lord. She is enlisted into the army of Israel, which has struggled over centuries to assert its identity and claim its territory. Unlike the traditional training a soldier undergoes, which is designed to build a hardness in battle and to suppress feelings of sympathy for one's enemies, Judith's "training" consists in prayer and, next to God, she is loyal to her people. She sets aside feelings for her own safety and risks everything for the sake of the nation.

Judith's heroism is allied to her cleverness in devising a plan to literally decapitate the head of the enemy. She has even thought about its aftermath, in particular the need for the Israelites to attack and defeat the Assyrian army. Yet the cool and calculated way in which she goes about her deed raises interesting spiritual and psychological questions. The way of holiness has led her to murder. What were the alternatives? If the Israelites had surrendered to the Assyrians, as their leaders had planned, their fate was uncertain. Judith has God's warrant to use extraordinary methods to bring about the desired end, at least for the Israelites. God is extolled by his people, and Judith's deep faith allows her to deflect the potential danger to her soul.

There are some interesting details which lead the reader into a deeper appreciation of Judith's character and what she underwent in order to fulfill her mission. First, her attachment to God, which may have increased following the death of her husband Manasseh, meant that she viewed her own actions in terms of a partnership with God. How did God assist her? Arguably, God's hand can be detected in the way that Holofernes became so drunk that he fell asleep, and also in the way that those around him faded into the night, leaving Holofernes alone with Judith and her maid. On the other hand, God does not make the actual killing of Holofernes easy. There is a detail about the description of his murder—that the first blow of the sword was not enough—which indicates that it was a proper butchering. God tests Judith's resolve and determination to carry through with her plan, no matter how messy.

Second, upon her return to Bethulia, Judith proudly boasts that Holofernes had "committed no sin with me, to defile and shame me." (Judith 13:16) Yet if Holofernes had not got drunk and passed out, but instead had seduced Judith as he had planned, then one must assume that Judith would have readily submitted to Holofernes' advances. By that stage, in her own mind, she had already subverted the moral underpinnings in her own character, by her deception and intention to commit murder. Sleeping with Holofernes would have been entirely consistent with her original plan.

When the Assyrians are defeated, the Israelites plunder their camp and bring home possessions for themselves. Judith is given the tent of Holofernes and all of his beds, bowls and furniture—she had already brought home the canopy over his bedchamber. All of it is dedicated to God, and the canopy is given as a votive offering: that is to say, Judith makes a gift of the canopy to God, in appreciation of the favor God has shown her. In the light of all that Judith has undergone, one wonders if this is equally an act of healing as of gratitude.

Judith has been compared to a number of other characters in the Bible, including Jael, Miriam, Deborah, Esther, Susanna and Ruth. In the final analysis, however, perhaps the character she resembles more than any other is Abraham. In obedience to the will of God, Abraham takes his son Isaac onto the mountain of Moriah, where he prepares a makeshift altar on which to sacrifice his son. (Genesis 22) As Abraham raises a dagger to take his son's life, an angel intervenes and Isaac is spared. In the same way, when Judith seeks to fulfill God's will, it leads her into the probability of sexual relations with Holofernes. Yet God spares her from this trial, which would defile her and would also defile the memory of her husband. Both Abraham and Judith are tested by God, and both come through, although there is an unspoken psychological cost to their obedience. The aftermath for both is comparable. Abraham offered a ram as a burnt offering; Judith made a votive offering of Holofernes' canopy.

In the final chapter, Judith is "honored throughout the whole country." (Judith 16:21) She never remarries (despite numerous suitors) and, when she dies, she is buried in the cave of her husband Manasseh. In her life she has experienced love and death, peace and war, holiness and violence. By seeking to do God's will, she exemplifies, in her own way, those who are called to be servants of God. If God calls his servants in love, then Judith shows us that courage and cunning can be weapons of love, especially when the survival of the nation is at stake. Throughout her story Judith cleaved close to God, praying to him, giving thanks and ascribing her victory to him. This story is as much about God as it is about Judith: it tells us that God is faithful to those who truly honor and serve him and that, in certain situations, God will test them to extremes.

QUESTIONS FOR REFLECTION:

1. Name some of the ways that God tests our faith.
2. If you were a novelist or scriptwriter, what backstory would you create for Judith?
3. The saying, "Everything is fair in love and war" seems to apply to Judith's story. Do you agree with this saying?
4. In the Bible there are several songs attributed to women: Hannah (1 Samuel 2:1-10), Deborah, (Judges 5) Mary (Luke 1:46-55), Judith (16:1-17.) What song resonates for you today?

CHAPTER 13

Samson

The Call to Fight

Among the Judges who ruled Israel following the death of Joshua, probably the most famous is Samson. Like many leaders of Israel before and since, he was called by God to fight against the Philistines. There is no one in the Bible quite like him. Possessing superhuman strength and a rampant libido, Samson is a child of nature whose wild and tragic story is a mixture of manly heroics and love betrayed.

Not surprisingly, few people today hold Samson up as a model of religious leadership. He is not the calm, reflective type popular with modern readers. Samson's strengths lie in other areas, particularly those of sex and combat. Samson is the action figure par excellence, a testosterone-fueled one-man army who takes the fight to the Philistines and wins. What is remarkable is that he does it all single-handedly. No wonder he is a hero to the people of Israel.

Samson appears at a time when the Lord had given Israel into the hands of its enemies, the Philistines. (Judges 13:1) The nation needed a savior: someone who could outwit the Philistines and defeat them in combat. The Lord gave them Samson, a Nazarite, a person consecrated to God for a special purpose.

Nazarites never cut their hair, which was thought to be the source of life, and they were forbidden alcohol so that the Spirit of God alone could determine their actions. (Number 6:2-21)

Samson's father was Manoah, from the tribe of Dan; we don't know the name of his mother. The couple are childless, but an angel of the Lord appears to Manoah's wife, telling her that she will give birth to a son who shall be a Nazarite. (Judges 13:3) The angel's appearance and message indicate that the fortunes of the couple, and of Israel, are about to change. The new savior of Israel will soon be born.

Manoah and his wife make a burnt offering to the Lord, and the angel appears again, this time in a fire, before ascending to heaven. (Judges 13:19-20) Samson is born, blessed by the Lord, and "the spirit of the Lord began to stir in him." (Judges 13:25) There is no account of Samson's early life, and when Samson is mentioned again, he is already an adult.

Samson's character is quickly established by the first words he utters. After noticing an attractive Philistine woman, he instructs his parents, "now get her for me as my wife." (Judges 14:2) Is Samson aware that Israelites are forbidden to intermarry? (to avoid the temptation to worship pagan gods). If so, it doesn't seem to matter to him. Samson is less concerned with laws and customs than with getting his own way. He insists on marriage, "because she pleases me." (Judges 14:3) The author of the story includes an explanatory note to let Samson off the hook: "this was from the Lord; for he was seeking a pretext to act against the Philistines." (Judges 14:4) It seems a little clumsy—in effect the author is saying that, in order to achieve his ends, God is prepared to break his own laws.

Later, Samson is out walking when he is surprised by a young lion, who roars at him. Samson reacts as "the spirit of the Lord rushed on him, and he tore the lion apart with his bare hands." (Judges 14:6) This incident tells us something about Samson and God. Samson is a kind of superhero, like Superman, whose power and strength is unlike any other. The story also shows God working through Samson in a purely physical way. Samson's wildness is emphasized once more when the rotting lion's carcass becomes a source of honey. Blithely disregarding the swarm of bees guarding it,

Jose Salome Pina, *Samson and Delilah*, 1851,
oil on canvas, Museo Nacional De Arte, Mexico City, Mexico

Samson scoops up the honey with his bare hands. Samson is perhaps the most purely masculine character in the Bible.

His assertive and powerful nature is also expressed in his relationships with women, all of which turn out to be problematic. The first woman he marries—the Philistine woman—betrays him over a riddle. After confronting the Philistines, (and employing a crude sexual innuendo in relation to his wife), Samson receives the spirit of the Lord and goes on the rampage.

> *He killed thirty Philistine men of the town, took their spoil,*
> *and gave the festal garments to those who had explained the*
> *riddle In hot anger, he went back to his father's house.*
> *(Judges 14:19)*

As for the woman, her father thought that Samson had rejected her, and so he gave her to Samson's best man. When Samson returns to visit his wife, he finds out that she has been given to another. What follows is a truly bizarre episode where Samson, in his anger, catches 300 foxes, ties their tails together, and sets them on fire. (Judges 15:4) The foxes burn the cornstores and vineyards of the Philistines. Because he feels he has been wronged, Samson says, "When I do mischief to the Philistines, I will be without blame." (Judges 15:3)

This is the beginning of a period of tit-for-tat violence. In retaliation for the murder of the thirty men, the Philistines take Samson's wife and her father and literally burn them alive. Samson takes revenge by striking the Philistines down "with great slaughter." Again, Samson's philosophy is summed up in his own words: "As they did to me, so I have done to them." (Judges 15:11) After the slaughter, he goes and lives in a cave.

Meanwhile, the Philistines continue to be a problem for the Israelites in Judah. Despite Samson's strength and his defeat of the Philistines, the men of Judah do not feel safe under his leadership. Therefore, they make a deal with the Philistines, which involves tying Samson up with rope and handing him over to the Philistines. Surprisingly, Samson goes along with the plan. As the men lead the bound Samson to the Philistines, we can guess what happens next. He breaks his bindings and kills a thousand of them, using the jaw of a donkey. This is an added insult to the Philistines, since a donkey was considered a lowly animal. The place of the massacre is called Jawbone Height. (Judges 15:18)

After the battle, Samson is spent. He prays to God for water to quench his thirst. His prayer is the opposite of the kind of humble entreaty typically offered in Scripture. He simply asks God a question, although his tone is sarcastic. He says,

> *You have granted this great victory by the hand of your servant. Am I now to die of thirst, and fall into the hands of the uncircumcised?*
>
> *(Judges 15:18)*

This is the first time that Samson describes himself, and the term he uses is servant. However, it is ironic that it is Samson who treats God like a servant. What is also remarkable is how God immediately accommodates Samson's wishes, as water bursts forth from the ground.

At this point in the story, we learn that Samson judged Israel for 20 years. The author picks up the story again when Samson visits Gaza and has sex with a prostitute. Shortly thereafter he meets the woman with whom he will be forever associated: Delilah. Her name means "flirty", which can also be a play on the words for *layela*, meaning night, compared to Samson's name which derives from *semes*, meaning sun.

Samson falls in love with a woman who does not love him back. The Philistines realize that they have an opportunity to defeat their apparently invincible opponent. They persuade Delilah to betray Samson, by offering to pay her 1100 shekels of silver about 275 times the price of a slave if she can discover the secret of his strength. She asks Samson to tell her, but he protects himself by giving her wrong answers. She persists, however, and

...after she had nagged him with her words, day after day, and pestered him, he was tired to death. So, he told her his whole secret.

(Judges 16:16-17)

The secret of Samson's strength is his hair. Delilah immediately informs the Philistine leaders who lie in wait for an opportunity to seize him. When he falls asleep in Delilah's lap, she shaves off the seven locks of his head. The weakened Samson is now easily overwhelmed by the Philistines, who bind him and gouge out his eyes (Judges 16:21)

It is a shocking turn in the story, and Samson is humiliated further by being put to work, shackled like an animal grinding at the prison mill. He spends all day going round and round – going nowhere, in fact. It is notable that during this time there is no attempt by the Israelites to rescue their leader. Was it fear of the Philistines that prevented them? Was it their own weakness, or were the people ambivalent about having Samson as their leader?

That could have been the end of the story, but there is one final twist. The Philistines have decided to celebrate the capture of Samson by offering a sacrifice to Dagon, their god. They decide to call Samson to perform for them, and make him stand between two pillars. As Samson's hands touch the pillars either side of him, he prays to God.

Lord God, remember me and strengthen me only this once, O God, so that with this one act of revenge I may pay back the Philistines for my two eyes.

(Judges 16:28)

Once again, God answers Samson's prayer immediately, and Samson pushes apart the pillars, killing himself and "more Philistines than he had killed during his life." (Judges 16:30) It is a suitably dramatic conclusion to an extraordinary life.

Where does one begin in evaluating the call of Samson to serve God? His call follows the familiar pattern of Jewish "saviors", who rescue the Israelites from their old enemy, the Philistines. What differentiates Samson from the others is his superhuman strength and the fantastical nature of his story. That one man can take on and defeat an army of thousands is not to be believed—not literally, anyway. How seriously, therefore, should we take him as a character?

To the Jews of the first century A.D., Samson was a hero. Even the sophisticated writer of the Letter to the Hebrews thought so and cited him admiringly as an example of a person of faith. (Hebrews 11:32-33) To modern readers, Samson seems like a familiar character from a Marvel Superhero movie, or like Moose Malloy in Raymond Chandler's *Farewell My Lovely*. The only surprise is that his story has not been updated for the movie-going public.

His betrayal by a woman, Delilah—a *femme fatale*—allows us to feel sympathy for him. It is interesting to note that in Samson's male-dominated world, Delilah appears to be of independent means. She is not described as the "wife of" or "daughter of" anyone. She captivates him and, through her persistence, is successful in discovering the secret of his strength.

Despite the parallels in modern culture, Samson's story is about more than love and sex. He is the leader of his people—he judged Israel for twenty years—and faithfully fulfills his calling to serve God to the end of his life. His imperfections are writ large and, although blessed with great strength, he has little subtlety or nuance. He seems only to be motivated by his sex drive and a desire for vengeance, and breaks his Nazarite obligations by chasing after foreign women. In one sense, he symbolizes the Israelites, who abandon God's law to worship idols.

Leaving aside Samson's macho exploits, what is striking about this story is the almost total absence of any support for Samson from his own people. In fact, the leaders of Judah are convinced that Samson is as much the cause of their woes as are the Philistines. (Judges 15:9-13) Nonetheless, Samson sees it as his duty—as one called by God—to protect and free them from the Philistines.

Whenever he describes himself, Samson says that he is a servant of God. Regardless of his success in the battlefield (and off), not once does Samson boast about his exploits. Although one can think of leaders who exercise and exemplify the traits of leadership in a more satisfying and rounded way, God has chosen this brutish and unsubtle man to serve him and to fight for his people. Samson's faith never seems to waiver, even when he is reduced to grinding at the mill in prison. In times of need, he knows where to turn for help, and God shows him mercy.

His final victory—one involving self-sacrifice—points to the victory of a future savior of Israel, Jesus Christ. When Samson prays to God, he is given strength to push apart the pillars of the Philistines' house, resulting in his own death along with the deaths of thousands of Philistines. However, the victory is framed within the old understanding of "an eye for an eye, a tooth for a tooth." However gratifying, taking revenge over one's enemies is like an endless spiral. How does one break free? For that, you need another kind of savior.

QUESTIONS FOR REFLECTION:

1. The story describes how, at the end of his life, Samson's weakness brings about Israel's deliverance. What are the ways in which God uses our strengths and weaknesses?
2. What kind of leader was Samson? There are times when leaders like Samson come to the fore. Why does God call Samson?
3. Are there current day equivalents of Samson in our own culture?
4. Compare Samson to Jesus. How do we reconcile the spiritual and natural forces in our lives? (See also Romans 8)

CHAPTER 14

Mary
The Call to Motherhood

The ancient priory of San Marco, in Florence, Italy, was once home to a thriving community of Dominican monks. It is now a museum, cherished for its beautiful Renaissance frescoes.

The artist responsible for the frescoes is the monk Fra Angelico, who lived for a time in the priory. Fra Angelico was a painter of great skill and refinement and completed a large number of religious paintings and frescoes. They remain among the most spiritual and inspiring works of Renaissance art.

The priory dates from the fifteenth century, when it was rebuilt by Cosimo De'Medici, who reserved a cell within for himself. Frescos of the patron, St. Dominic, loom over the visitor in many places around the priory. He is usually present in the paintings of the crucifixion. He also appears in small frescoes with his finger pressed against his lips, enjoining those present to silence. He reminds us that monastic discipline requires the avoidance of idle chatter and, in its place, an inward dialogue with God.

Among the former residents of San Marco was the ascetic monk Fra Girolamo Savonarola, famous for his fiery sermons against cultural decadence, and for the "Bonfire of the Vanities", the destruction of those objects deemed a danger to Christian piety:

musical instruments, cosmetics, manuscripts, playing cards, and paintings.

Savonarola would have been familiar with Fra Angelico's frescoes, painted fifty years earlier. At the top of the staircase which connects the chapel with the monks' cells, Fra Angelico's most famous fresco, the Annunciation, would have been seen daily by every monk of the community. The fresco is large, about 7½ feet by 10½ feet. It is one of a number of versions of this scene that Fra Angelico painted.

The picture depicts the moment when Mary, as a young girl, is visited by the angel Gabriel. The encounter is recorded in Luke's gospel.

> *In the sixth month, the angel Gabriel was sent by God to a town in Galilee called Nazareth, to a virgin engaged to a man whose name was Joseph, of the house of David. The virgin's name was Mary. And he came to her and said, "Greetings, favored one! The Lord is with you." But she was much perplexed by his words and pondered what sort of greeting this might be. The angel said to her, "Do not be afraid, Mary, for you have found favor with God. And now, you will conceive in your womb and bear a son, and you will name him Jesus. He will be great, and will be called the Son of the Most High, and the Lord God will give to him the throne of his ancestor David. He will reign over the house of Jacob forever, and of his kingdom, there will be no end." Mary said to the angel, "How can this be since I am a virgin?" The angel said to her, "The Holy Spirit will come upon you, and the power of the Most High will overshadow you; therefore the child to be born will be holy; he will be called Son of God. And now, your relative Elizabeth in her old age has also conceived a son; and this is the sixth month for her who was said to be barren. For nothing will be impossible with God." Then Mary said, "Here am I, the servant of the Lord; let it be with me according to your word." Then the angel departed from her.*
>
> *(Luke 1:26-38)*

Fra Angelico, *Annunciation*, c. 1438-1450,
fresco, 7 ½ ft. by 10 ½ ft. , Museo del Convento di San Marco, Florence, Italy

Mary is a young girl, thought to have been around 13 or 14 years old when the angel Gabriel appears to her. At the time she was betrothed to an older man named Joseph.

In the painting, Mary's hands are folded protectively across her body. Her face shows apprehension, but she leans forward in order to hear what the angel is saying. The angel also leans forward, almost genuflecting before the young girl. The angel's hands are also folded across his body, mirroring the pose of the virgin. It is a scene of graceful tension.

Mary is chosen by God to conceive and bear God's son. Why did God choose Mary? She held neither rank nor royal title nor was she the daughter of a High Priest. Her hometown, Nazareth, was little regarded, as the comment of the disciple Nathanael indicates. (John 1:46) Although her fiancé was descended from the line of David, as many were, there is nothing else to make us think that Mary was chosen for any other reason than that her inward disposition made her suitable. It was something innate that determined that God would choose her for this sacred calling.

From the gospel of Luke, it is possible to infer that she already had an interior life and was a person of faith. Although she is frightened by the appearance of the angel, she has the presence of mind to question him. She never stops and says: "This can't be happening to me," or "God has surely made a mistake." She takes God's call seriously, and even questions how a virgin can conceive without first being with a man.

With great patience the angel explains the purpose of his visit, telling Mary that she will bear the "Son of the Most High", and that with God nothing is impossible. When Mary absorbs Gabriel's message she replies with these famous and impressive words: "Here am I, the servant of the Lord; let it be with me according to your word." This translation doesn't quite convey the sense that Mary, in agreeing to bear God's son, is submitting her will entirely to God. A more literal translation, from David Bentley Hart, conveys this better. Mary says:

> *See the slave of the Lord [doulē Kyriou]; may it happen to me as you have said[1].*

Mary's reply highlights her willingness to be God's slave. The term "slave" is problematic for us today. When the gospels were written, slavery was common—at least one in four people were slaves—and slavery was embedded in the economic system of the Roman Empire. Mary's response therefore identifies her as among the lowest in the economic order. At the same time, it emphasizes unambiguously her total surrender to the will of God. However, this surrender is not an admission of defeat, nor is Mary saying that she will be God's puppet. Her surrender is to be understood as the continuance of a pre-existing relationship. Only now, God is deepening that relationship.

Mary trusts God with faith and humility. The feeling is mutual, for we can say, too, that God trusts Mary. Here we reach the heart of the call to love and what it means. Mary trusts God. God trusts Mary. In this relationship, there is no clear line dividing heaven and earth. Instead earth and heaven are merged and, in the process, Mary's soul is transformed: she says, "My soul magnifies the Lord." (Luke 1:46) This is the power of faith as a magnifier, an enlarger. Love has no barriers. As St. Ambrose once said about Mary's wonderful prayer, "Let Mary's soul be in us to glorify the Lord; let her spirit be in us that we may rejoice in God our Savior."

Mary is called to motherhood. It is the cause of both joy and suffering. Mary will experience the joy of bringing new life into the world and of making a family home. She will also experience displacement and suffering because of her son: she will go into exile, far away from her own family, and then watch her son grow up and become independent of her. Finally, she will see him die. At Jesus's crucifixion, the prophecy of Simeon, "And a sword shall pierce your own heart" (Luke 2:35) will come true for her.

Mary is mentioned sparingly in the Scriptural accounts; it is easier to talk about what makes her significant than to say what sort

[1] David Bentley Hart, *The New Testament* (Yale: Yale University Press, 2017) p. 105

of person she was. In Luke's gospel she hears the shepherds' story and "treasures all these words and pondered them in her heart." (Luke 2:19) This hints at her reflective nature and confirms her interior life. At the wedding in Cana she directs the steward with an instruction which echoes her own affirmation, when she says, "Do whatever he tells you." (Luke 2:5) She is faithful to her son throughout his life and then stays with the Church which Christ has founded.

When most people think of Mary, it is usually at Christmas time, when the churches have their crèche and Mary is played by a young child holding a baby Jesus. The Christmas pageant attracts a large congregation of doting parents and grandparents who come to see their children and grandchildren re-enacting the Nativity story. This innocent and heart-warming event is actually proclaiming an astounding event in human history: God has become a human being, and his name is Jesus, meaning "the one who saves." Salvation has come to birth at Christmas.

The setting of Jesus' birth, in the humble manger at Bethlehem, allows us to focus on the family group of Jesus, Mary and Joseph. When Mary gives birth, it is an event hidden from the rest of the world. Mary's own family is absent on what should be an occasion of joy. There is no one there to aid her apart from Joseph. In her separation from family and festival, Mary shows the resilience of her nature, which is not one of superhuman emotional strength, but of reliance on her husband and God for support.

In the poverty and strangeness of her surroundings, God is present. In fact, God wants to emphasize how his plan for Mary and for all humanity will be manifest: in the pure expression of love, undistracted by wealth, opulence, or even family tradition. God has reserved this place and time for Mary and Joseph together. By reducing everything to its most basic elements, God focuses our attention on the family which is united in love. The holy family is an example of the harmony, unity, and stability that we sense is the key to a godly life.

When we imagine the scene in the manger, the picture it provides is one of mutual enrichment, vulnerability, and support. It illustrates how salvation is found in family and community life. People of faith work out their Christian vocation in the company of others, not only in Church but outside of it, in service to others, and in following Christ and allowing him into our life—into every part of it. This works to our best advantage when we make ourselves simple followers, like Mary, concentrating first on our relationship with God and then on the needs of others. Cardinal Walter Kasper wrote that

Mary is an example, a model, a type of our discipleship. God wants our Yes in response to his Yes; God wants us to be inspired, sustained, and empowered by his grace—co-workers and co-operators in his salvific work. Saint Augustine put it: "He who has created us without us, does not redeem us without us." Every one of us has his or her personal vocation and mission, his or her personal charisma, everybody has his or her place.[2]

The cardinal's words remind us that Christ's call is a universal one. Mary's example of humility, trust, and acceptance is the prototype of our response to God's call in our own lives. Like Mary, we can be favored by God, and together with her form a community of grace that will spread throughout the world.

Mary learned that when God comes to you, wherever you happen to be, you will need to decide how to respond. You will understand that God values you and has an intention for you. He has called you in love, and to love in return. Our souls were created for this kind of love which we sometimes describe as "spiritual", but which is really the growth of the heart to love as God loves, which is to love without measure and to love freely.

That is the call for God's faithful, to surrender to God, like Mary, and to become part of his plan of salvation. Mary offered herself in humility and, through the action of the Holy Spirit, allowed Christ to be formed in her.

[2] Walter Kasper, "Mary and the Unity of the Church", in *Mary: A Focus of Unity for all Christians?* (Norfolk: CBS, 2009) p. 45

QUESTIONS FOR REFLECTION:

1. In most translations of the Annunciation, Mary calls herself a "handmaid" or "servant" of the Lord. Yet, the literal meaning is "slave." How do these two different definitions shape our understanding of Mary's response?

2. Consider the personal implications of Mary's "yes" to God. How might her life be affected?

3. Mary is a model of humility. C. S. Lewis said that "Humility is not thinking less of yourself, but of thinking about yourself less often." What is the role of humility in God's call to love?

4. Many people find it difficult to trust in God absolutely. How do we learn to trust in God?

Part III
The Contemporary Call

CHAPTER 15

Christopher

The Call to Live

In 1988 I was living in the British seaside town of Brighton. I attended St. Michael and All Angels church, where I was in charge of the Sunday school and editor of the church magazine. The church was built in Victorian times and imitated the grand style of Roman churches. It had a high rood screen, and an interior east end wall made entirely of marble. The stained-glass windows were pre-Raphaelite, and dotted around the expansive interior were a series of altars dedicated to various saints.

Known as the "cathedral of the back streets", St. Michael's was a jewel in an otherwise ordinary Brighton Street. The Rector at the time was Father Freddie Jackson, an ascetic and celibate priest who had a devotion to the Mass unlike any I have known before or since. The congregation was lively and friendly, and welcoming to newcomers. I worshipped there for eighteen years, during which time I made a number of new friends. One of these was Christopher.

When Christopher arrived at St. Michael, he was unknown to most of us, but we soon learned his story. Christopher had experienced a reversal of fortune, as he describes in an article he wrote for the church magazine:

I was released from HMP Winchester, at the end of April 1988 after serving a sentence of a year for a substantial tax fraud. In practice, such relatively short sentences are subject to a 50% remission, itself subject to good behavior and this applied in my case, and I was on the 'IN' for only six months. Quite long enough for me—a very sharp lesson indeed and, while I breathe, never ever to be repeated.

Christopher was married and had four children, all of whom had left home (the eldest, Rupert, was mentally disabled and spent his life in an institution). Christopher had enjoyed several advantages in life: he attended the elite Rugby Public School as a boy, and his family had provided for him in his early years. Tall and with a natural charm, he made friends easily. With his slightly shabby tweed jacket and pipe, which he smoked on social occasions, he was, in many ways, from another time.

His conviction for fraud had undone him. He had lost his living, his home, and his marriage. A tragedy such as this would have broken a lesser man, but Christopher decided to make the best of it. He knew very well that he was the author of his own downfall, and that to wallow in self-pity would serve no purpose.

Life after prison would be very different from life before. He had lost contact with many of his former friends. Expensive dinners on the firm's tab were a thing of the past. Instead, his weekly allowance from the government enabled him to rent a room in a house and live frugally from week to week.

Christopher was a member of Alcoholics Anonymous. His drinking had been a part of his life before prison. After prison, he never drank again, although on one occasion he was tempted. He recounts what happened:

It was Christmas 1991. I was on my own feeling rather mournful and having a small wallow in self-pity—that enemy of us all!—and opened a gift-wrapped bottle given to me by a generous if misguided friend for what I had supposed to be a bottle of cordial turned out to be one of

Gordon's gin. I looked at this massive enticement and suddenly was in the throes of a devastating 'wobble' i.e. panic attack, began to shake and sweat, my stomach cramped and for one awesome moment I thought I was in for an attack of the 'horrors' when you think you are being chased by pink elephants all madly trumpeting, and I knew I stood at a personal crossroads. I prayed intently and then knocked the top off the bottle and spilt the contents down the sink—glass everywhere as there simply wasn't time to get the top off. I heaved a sigh of relief, drank a pint of milk, and went to two AA meetings in succession as of course I knew where and when these were being held at such potentially difficult times as Christmas.

In AA he became a mentor to those who were going through the process of quitting. He was an effective mentor, as far as I could tell. He told me of members who rang him during the night when they were tempted to pick up the bottle and start drinking again. Christopher would offer encouraging advice in his cultured voice and was not above salting his ministrations with choice language. When people were wavering, that was an effective way to get the message across, he told me.

He was a shrewd observer of human nature, especially when judging the characters of others. As a former convict, he had a good eye for identifying crooks and those who were not as they appear to be, even among our church congregation. Prison had robbed him of any illusions about his own importance, and his lack of ego helped him to rub along with most people. He had served part of his time in Lewes Prison, where he had the job of sewing mailbags alongside Reggie Kray, the London gangster.

Christopher had a social side, and we met for lunch often, either at the Ship or the Sussex pub, where we would end up talking about our lives, the church, or my own calling to ministry. He met my parents once when they were visiting from New Zealand. My mother, another shrewd judge of human character, described Christopher as an old *roué*. He seemed to have lady friends in various parts of the country. When I went to theological college in

Yorkshire in 2007 to train for the ministry, he wrote to let me know how much he would miss my company, and in passing mentioned a "close lady friend" who lived in the county, with whom he stayed several times.

The letter he sent me contains much that made Christopher so endearing. It is hand-written in his beautiful style, and displays his eclectic interests. He mentioned that he hoped to meet with a church couple for lunch; Christopher and the husband shared an interest in steam locomotives. The letter contains an account of an autumn bazaar at St. Andrews, an article from the Daily Telegraph about the fall in the stock market, and a note about the current fees for Eton College (£26,500 in 2007).

Christopher's curiosity about people and things was one of the secrets of his survival. When he left prison, he could have turned again to drink, but instead chose sobriety. He sought out the company of others, relying upon his gifts for friendship and conversation to give meaning to his new life. He signaled the changes in his life by reclaiming his original name, Christopher, rather than continuing with his nickname, Kit. The name change was a way of separating himself from his past. Kit was the *bon viveur*, the charmer who was stealing from the firm and living the high life. By contrast, Christopher was living in straitened circumstances, with no reputation to speak of. However, the church welcomed him, and he found among its members a supportive and non-judgmental community.

Outside every church, there should be a sign saying "Sinners Welcome." Christopher certainly counted himself among them. He attended church regularly and I was there when, at the end of Mass one Sunday, the parish priest announced the need for a campaign to raise money for roof repairs. I can still remember the stunned silence among the congregation when we heard how much it would cost: £402,000. That was enough to build three new churches, I thought. My next thought was, where on earth were we to get the money from?

There was an established group called the "Friends of St. Michael's", who could contribute. Retired and well-connected clergy in the parish could be counted on to ask friends and acquaintances to put some money in. There would be a mailing campaign to members and to various people and organizations. However, someone was needed to run the campaign and to deal with donations and correspondence. Christopher stepped forward, and volunteered to be the "point person." An office was created in a room off the church, with a desk, computer, and telephone line.

On behalf of the church, Christopher wrote countless letters requesting donations, sending thanks when they arrived, and making phone calls. He was in the office most days and applied himself conscientiously to the role. The raising of the monies for repairs took over two years and was considerably helped by grants from English Heritage and the European Commission. Thanks to the efforts of many people, the church eventually raised the money, and the necessary repairs were undertaken. Christopher's contribution was his time and himself, making it possible for the church to have a continuous and responsive contact in the long process of fundraising.

His role expanded to include much of the basic running of the church—what today we would call a parish administrator. In those days, most clergy in the Church of England dealt with the paperwork from their vicarages or rectories. In creating an "office"—a particular place where people could drop in—the church was also creating a new ministry. Christopher, with his gregarious nature, fitted the role perfectly. He raised money for the church but also welcomed the "regulars" who came in for a chat, and those who were coming to church for the first time.

I think that Christopher found a "calling" within the church, almost by accident, in the role of administrator. It got him out of bed in the morning and focused his gifts toward the goal of meeting the church's needs. Perhaps it was also a kind of reparation for what he had done; the money that passed through his hands was not for his own pleasure, but for the good of the church—for the glory of God. Our parish priest had a habit of placing convicted offenders in places of trust—a risky prospect, but where Christopher was concerned, it paid off.

Christopher remained poor for the rest of his life, yet he had a rich and diverse circle of acquaintances: Christopher's other calling was to friendship. I met some of his housemates where he lived. All of them were single men who were living week to week on welfare. Christopher befriended and encouraged them all, and acted as a kind of father figure to them.

I kept in contact with Christopher until the end of his life. As his health began to fail, he stepped down from the role of administrator at the church. We continued to meet regularly for lunch, usually at one of the local pubs, near where he lived. He told me that he wished that he and his wife could patch things up and make another go of it, but it never happened. However, there was a reconciliation of sorts and, by the end, they were both talking to each other again. His daughters too, were in touch, and I got to meet them both.

I met his second son Humphrey a few times when he came to church. He was like his father, with the same bluff manner. He lived and worked in the USA, and had an American girlfriend. Sadly tragedy struck when, at the age of 48, Humphrey suffered a traumatic head injury in a car crash. Two months later, while in Ireland, he died of a brain hemorrhage. Christopher was devastated and wrote to me lamenting the loss of his son. Everyone who knew Christopher rallied around to give him support, prayers, and whatever else we could provide. While nothing could take away the grief he felt, he received much sympathy and help from those who loved him. In such situations churches become families, and our Christian brothers and sisters provide us with the love and strength to carry on.

That sense of "family" became apparent to me when I headed off to theological college in Mirfield, West Yorkshire, in the fall of 2007. Christopher and I continued to write to each other, although he was a better letter writer than I was. He always signed off his letters as a variation of "yours ever" or "your friend." However, in the last letter I have from him, dated September 20, he signs off as "Ever yours with the love of a father for his son."

Four months after writing that letter, I received the sad news that Christopher had died. I drove down from Yorkshire for the funeral, and my two sons, who knew Christopher from our pilgrimages to Walsingham, attended with me. At the funeral there seemed to be two groups of people in the church: those who knew "Kit", the man of means and status; and then there were those who, like me, knew Christopher as the engaging but humble man who created for himself a new life in the church and the AA, and who discovered a calling there.

In his life, Christopher showed the importance of character—even one as flawed as his own. He never gave up, despite his world collapsing around him. When he seemed to have lost everything—his job, marriage, and reputation—he decided that life still had something to offer. Or perhaps, he still had something to offer life. His prison experience had given him time to reflect on his actions and on what kind of person the future Christopher would be like. He became a friend, mentor, and father to many. His life was a kind of resurrection, and I pray he now enjoys peace and joy in the resurrection life with Jesus Christ.

CHAPTER 16

Norah

The Call to Pray

When I was discerning a call from God, the conversations I had with clergy usually revolved around whether or not I had a vocation to the priesthood. The notion of being called by God was thus exclusively related to ordained ministry. To answer God's call, and set a course to becoming a priest, would involve a re-orienting of my life and identity. Once I had committed to this path, my life was no longer my own, but God's.

There seemed to be a clear distinction between this type of call, with its requirement for radical change, and the call to serve in other capacities. For example, those who worked in the church office or who cooked the Saturday breakfasts were not expected to relate to what they did as a "calling," but simply as an offering of their time and talents.

This distinction between ordained ministry and other forms of service rests on the Hebrew understanding of a priest being "holy" that is, being "set apart" for a specific purpose. (Exodus 29:33 and Leviticus 21) The clergy are distinct from the laity, although the relationship between both is designed to be complementary. Both are sheep under the one shepherd, Jesus Christ, but the priest is Christ's shepherd on earth. This symbolism is made explicit by the crozier—the shepherd's crook—carried by the bishop.

Yet it is possible to enlarge the meaning of "calling" beyond the call to holy orders. God's call goes out to anyone who is attentive to the word of God and who is willing to serve. The call will usually come through a request from the priest to take on a particular task or church ministry. The questions "Can you sing in the choir?" or "Can you help out in the office once a week?" will be familiar to anyone who is a regular churchgoer. It seems rather grand to describe these activities as "callings," but the same principle of service underlies this kind of work as it does the work of a deacon or priest.

Much of the conversation around calling focuses on the merging of divine and human wills, and how this relates to one's history and faith journey. Another significant factor is that of "place"—of being in the right place at the right time. Some places—not always churches—seem to act as hotspots for spiritual life and development, producing a higher number of those called than anywhere else. A famous example is Holy Trinity, Brompton, London, which developed and promoted the Alpha course. From the 1990's onward, church attendance grew significantly and now reaches 4,500 every Sunday, across several churches.

My own experience of being in the right place at the right time occurred during an eighteen-year period at the church of St. Michael and All Angels, Brighton, England, during which time I, and four other members, discerned a call to ordained ministry. This call was one that emerged over a period of time. I doubt that it would have gone as far as it did, had I not met Norah, who was a member of St. Michael's at that time. She was to have a decisive and abiding influence on my future path in life.

Norah lived on Victoria Street, about three minutes' walk from the church, in a house owned by her son. She had been married four times but had no financial resources to speak of. She had no car, but within the compact environs of the town she was fit enough to walk everywhere.

When I first met her, she always seemed to be in church. Indeed, whenever I hear the story of the Presentation, and of the prophetess

Anna, I think of Norah. Every morning at 7:30 am, Norah would come to church and sit in stillness before the Blessed Sacrament, the consecrated body of Christ which was reserved in the tabernacle. At 8:00 am she would then take part in the first Mass of the day.

She subscribed to a magazine called Retreat, which was a nationwide directory of retreat houses. She usually left a copy of the magazine at the back of the church for anyone to read. One day I picked up the magazine and, as I was reading it, Norah walked by. I told her I was interested in going on retreat. Could she recommend anywhere? She looked at me doubtfully and asked,

"Have you ever been on retreat before?" "No," I replied, "but I would like to try."

"It may not be for you. I mean, what if you get there and then, after an hour, you decide that you don't like it? You've booked for a three-night stay."

I insisted that I was still interested.

"I have another idea," she countered, "why not try Christian meditation? That's only half an hour. It might help you to know if a retreat is right for you."

The meditation she referred to was that practiced and promoted by the Dominican monk John Main, who re-introduced meditation to mainstream Christianity. There was a meditation group that met every Monday evening, in the living room of a Roman Catholic convent in Preston Park, Brighton. Norah invited me to join the group one evening.

The group was a mixture of Catholics and Anglicans. Its leader was Paul, who was in his thirties. The group would sit in chairs in the room and listen to a recording of John Main, whose gentle and steady voice set the tone for the evening. John Main talked about how to meditate, and the importance of the spiritual life. The talks usually lasted around ten minutes. They were followed by a short excerpt of music, and then we began to meditate.

On first acquaintance, Christian meditation sounds very simple: all you do is repeat the Aramaic word *maranatha*, silently, for 25 minutes. I soon found out that "simple" does not equate to "easy." As I tried to focus my attention on the word, I found my thoughts drifting off into other areas related to my life: work, family, and plans for the next day. I returned again and again to the mantra, as John Main suggested, and it seemed to be working until my attention was diverted again. I meditated for 25 minutes. And so it went, week after week, day after day. I began to meditate every morning and every evening. It was right for me.

Meditation became a discipline that changed my life. Through meditation, my faith became deeper. On Sunday mornings I was hearing things in the readings that I had never noticed before. The gospel crackled with new meaning, and I began to attend daily Mass.

The meditation group itself turned out to be a source of further unexpected blessings. I made lasting friendships with members of the group. Years later, one of them allowed me to live in his house for a while when I had nowhere to live. Another was the best man at my wedding.

Norah was delighted to see my transformation because it was one she had undergone herself. At St. Michael's, Norah was encouraged by her parish priest, Father Freddie, to devote herself to prayer. Her daily time of quiet before Mass was actually a time of meditation. She had, in St. Augustine's words, a "holy desire" for God which had the effect of stretching her soul in order to increase its capacity. St. Augustine describes God pouring himself into one's soul, in order to replace its bitterness with God's sweetness.

It was this "holy desire" that led her to pray before the Blessed Sacrament. Her daily discipline, joyfully accepted, was, in effect, a form of adoration. This kind of prayer is what monastics describe as an "unmotivated, uninterrupted act of loving service." A priest once gave me an alternative definition: "I look at him and he looks at me." Norah looked at God, and in God's returning gaze she saw the life of God within and around her.

Norah attended daily Mass because it was irresistible. In the Eucharist, she received the holy sacrament of the body and blood of Christ, which fed and sustained her. As her love for God grew, her steady and faithful presence in church served as a persuasive example to the rest of us, to seek God in prayer. The joy of love—God's love—seemed to emanate from her.

Prayer was central to her life, but Norah was also a skillful calligrapher and artist, as well as a poet. She once showed me a picture that she had drawn and given to Father Freddie. In the middle of the picture was Christ in the Blessed Sacrament, and then the church, and then the town, and then the world. She wanted to show how our church had become a store of love which radiated into the streets and towns and world which surrounded us.

She gave me poems to print in the church magazine. One of them was personal, relating to a past event with her children, and a few days after giving me the poem she asked me not to include it. Another poem, inspired by a church candle with barbed wire twisted around its frame (the symbol for Amnesty International), was published in the March 1990 edition of the church magazine.

Holy Prisoner

Symbols of life within a prison cell
[The night light and the crab of twisted wire]
Have stirred in me a casual desire
To kneel and pray and wish the victim well.
But as I watch the gentle flicking flame
I feel a presence near me in the place
And, through the shadows, recognize the face
And hear the quiet whisper of my name.

My God, it is my God who lies so near,
Tortured and shackled, close to very death,
Sharing the hell, the agony and fear
Which men inflict on men throughout the earth.
Despite the ill that I have done to Thee
Dear Lord, turn not your face away from me.

As she grew older, Norah decided it was time to move from her three-story house on Victoria Street to a one level apartment. She placed her name on a waiting list to be accommodated at St. Mary's Hospital in Chichester—not a hospital in the modern sense, but a twelfth century almshouse dedicated to the Virgin Mary. It provided accommodation for Christian women of the diocese who had no resources and nowhere to live. Norah was delighted when, after a period of waiting, she was told that there was a small apartment available for her.

One weekend I took my two boys over to see her in her new home, and she showed us the inside of the building—it was unusual in that the apartments had walls but no ceilings; all of the apartments were under the one roof of the building. For this reason, no televisions were allowed, which didn't bother Norah as, like me, she didn't own one. Her apartment was just under the old clock which used to chime every hour. There was a chapel at the end of the building, where the Blessed Sacrament was reserved. When Norah couldn't sleep during the night, she could go into the chapel to pray.

I have a clear memory of the day of our visit, including a picnic on the lawn outside. I met the *custos*, or chaplain, Bishop Edward Knapp-Fisher, who signed a copy of his book *Belief and Prayer* for me, which I still have. On that day there was also a visit from sixty French tourists, who were being shown around by the bishop. I sent Norah a photo of us on the lawn and she replied with a postcard to my children, saying "I expect the French people enjoyed seeing you and your Dad, an English family enjoying themselves on an English lawn with buttercups and daisies!"

St. Mary's Hospital provided Norah with holy, simple and convenient accommodation. She also found a new church home at St. Wilfrid's, Chichester to replace St. Michael's, and seemed happy there. I saw her less frequently, as happens when people move away. Norah spent her final years in Chichester, and died peacefully.

St. Michael's continued, although after Father Freddie left, and then Norah, it was never the same as before. Looking back, it seems as though the Holy Spirit had decided to make a home a St.

Michael's during Norah's time. Like Anna in the Temple, she had seen the salvation of the Lord and it filled her with peace and joy. When people talk about the life of a church, they often refer to the many activities that its members undertake. However, I usually think of Norah, praying in church every day, inviting God to take a larger part in her spiritual life. God called her to this secret life, for her sake and for the sake of the church, as the Spirit moved through the church to revitalize and transform it. In that mysterious power that prayer has, Norah was the bringer of blessings beyond her own orbit, and an angel of God's grace.

CHAPTER 17

Everett

The Call to Serve

In conversation with Everett Gillison, I noticed how the call to serve occurs and re-occurs throughout his life. He is currently senior warden at the Church of the Holy Apostles and the Mediator, in Philadelphia, and Director of Employee and Labor Relations at the Defender's Office, also in Philadelphia. He has also been a social worker, lawyer, seminarian, Deputy Mayor for Public Safety in the city of Philadelphia from 2011-2016, Board Member of the Pennsylvania Department of Probation and Parole, and, last but not least, husband, son, and father to two daughters.

Everett's life has been centered in Philadelphia. He grew up in a time when American society was changing. The core values he received from his family—the need for integrity, having an honest work ethic and not waiting for things to come your way—helped the young Everett to navigate the turbulence of the 1960s and 70s and allowed him to take advantage of life's opportunities. Everett observes that, "In my family, there has always been responsibility and leadership, poured into me by others."

The family was originally from South Carolina, moving to Philadelphia in the 1920s as part of the Great Migration. They had experienced the effects of racism in the south and sought new opportunities in the north. In Philadelphia, they found a spiritual home at the Episcopal church of Holy Apostles and the Mediator. At the time, the neighborhood and church were mainly white. However, following the race riots of 1964, the racial profile of the neighborhood in West Philadelphia changed, as many white families moved out. The racial mix at church changed too, from white to mainly black in less than two years.

In the early 1970s, Everett attended a new high school— University City (now closed)—which opened the door to new possibilities. He realized that "As a young black man in America, you have to be driven because you can't be defined by what others see." As he matured, he understood that he was primarily responsible for his own learning. Not everyone could do that, he acknowledges, but with a certain amount of determination and discipline, he realized he could gain the skills and abilities that would equip him for his future career.

Among the first to graduate from the University City High School, Everett remembers what the school principal, Davis Martin, said to him: "I need you to be true to who you are. If you are true to who you are, you will do marvelous things." Martin encouraged his students to "seek the light."

Another early influence was Herman Wrice, who led a community organization that helped provide employment assistance to blacks yearning to improve their lot. Wrice said, "If you give young black men an opportunity they will be able to succeed." Drexel University agreed to test Wrice's proposition and asked for five candidates to study there. Wrice called Everett, and said to him, "I need you to go. You will be working with a professor at Drexel, and you will be part and parcel of this matter. Do your homework and do well."

After graduating with a B.A., Everett became a social worker, advocating for those who had fallen on the wrong side of the law. Some of those he helped were friends who had dropped out of school. Everett became their voice, "translating" for them in court. By taking on this work, Everett was making a clear statement about who he was and what his calling was. He explains, "I'm from the community. I understand. That's who I am."

At that time, he was not a lawyer and had no ambition to argue in front of judges. However, he was encouraged to see himself in this role, and in 1982 he eventually applied to and was accepted by Syracuse Law School. This was not to be the first time that Everett embarked on a future direction due to the promptings of others. Later, Bishop Franklin Turner would convince him to pursue a vocation to ordained ministry.

Everett graduated from law school and returned to Philadelphia and to the Public Defender's Office, where he worked for the next 26 years, as a trial attorney and advocate, "keeping people off death row." He rose through the ranks to become a member of the first Special Defense and Capital Homicide Unit in the City of Philadelphia.

While his career advanced, he was less involved in the church. He describes himself at that time as a CEMD Christian (Christmas, Easter, and Mother's Day). The rest of his family made up for Everett's absence: his mother (who is now in her nineties) and sisters were long-term vestry members and ran many of the church programs at Holy Apostles and the Mediator. Everett was married to Elaine there in 1988, and in 1992 their first child was born.

Three years later, Everett's relationship to the church, and to faith in general, was to change. Elaine was expecting twins, but there were complications, and it was discovered that one of the babies had died. The other survived, but she was born prematurely, by Caesarian section, and weighed about three pounds. During surgery, the doctors had cut two of the mother's organs and now she, along with the baby, were fighting for their lives. This crisis brought a "spiritual awakening" in Everett's life. He spent a week in the hospital praying for the recovery of his wife and child. Mercifully, both Elaine and the child survived. The experience proved a turning point in Everett's life.

He returned to the church and was appointed senior warden. Everett worked with interim priests until the church called a permanent rector in 1998. Around this time, Everett also began working with the Diocese of Pennsylvania, with Bishops Bartlett and Turner, in the finance and property department and in the diocesan mission. Suffragan Bishop Franklin Turner, an African American, saw Everett as a gift to the church, and kept talking to him about "formation." Everett recalls Turner telling him, "You have the talent, you know you have a call. You're smart enough to understand that there's a role for you as a priest. I want you to pray about this."

The bishop was not the only one encouraging Everett along this path. People at church were saying the same thing. Everett "prayed about it quite a lot." He quietly went on spiritual weekends and spent time at Daylesford Abbey. He and a friend spent four semesters at Seminary, learning more about the Bible and studying Greek and Hebrew. It seems as though the road to ordained ministry was stretching out ahead of him. Then something happened that stopped him in his tracks.

Bishop Turner had assigned Everett a spiritual director, Rev. Paula Lawrence-Wehmiller. Spiritual direction can be summarized as help given by one Christian to another, which enables that person to pay attention to God's personal communication to him or her, to grow in intimacy with God, and to live into the fullness of that relationship.

On one occasion, Rev. Paula asked Everett, "How does your wife feel about you doing this ministry?" He replied that Elaine had never objected. The spiritual director pressed him: "You don't see that your presence and what you want to do is so commanding. You need to create a space intentionally for your wife to speak. God put you guys together. You have to listen."

Everett took the advice and listened to his wife. He was shocked and genuinely surprised by what he heard. Elaine told him that she didn't want him to train for the ministry. If he did, it would mean he would have to quit his job. The couple had young children and she didn't want to leave home and spend a full year at General Seminary in New York. She told him bluntly, "You're doing this on your own."

Elaine's message caught Everett off guard. Giving up the chance to train at the Seminary seemed to be throwing away all the patient work of spiritual formation and preparation. Wasn't God calling him into ordained ministry? On the other hand, Everett now had a duty as a husband and father to Elaine and their two young children. It was unthinkable that he should separate himself from them to pursue the call to the priesthood, however noble such a call may be. After much soul searching, he decided to abandon the idea of going to seminary. Looking back, he admits that, at the time, "I wasn't really listening to everything that was going on around me."

The advice of his spiritual director, Rev. Paula Lawrence-Wehmiller, had taught a valuable lesson. No man is an island to himself. She gave him specific advice for his prayer life: he was to pray, not in general, but "to ask the Lord to close doors, not open them," she said, "because if you ask the Lord to open doors, you will get so many pathways and opportunities. You know, if you put to mind to anything, you will be able to do it. What you need is for God to show you the only and best way forward."

Two years later, in 2007, Everett decided that, even if training for the ministry was no longer on the table, he would at least complete his Master of Divinity. "I never started something I didn't finish." But that plan was put on hold when, out of the blue, he received a phone call from his friend, Michael Nutter, who had just been elected Mayor of the City of Philadelphia. Nutter asked Everett to be Deputy Mayor.

Everett remembers the conversation: "He told me, 'There's no one I trust more than you. I want you to join me as Deputy Mayor, because your perspective is sorely needed to get us in the right place.' And I was saying, 'I'm not a politician. I wouldn't like that kind of stuff.' And Nutter said, 'the police will report to you, the fire department will report to you, the office of emergency management, the prisons—you have done nothing but give your life to the poor and now I'm giving you the keys to try, to shift the focus, and to do all the things you told me I should be doing.'"

The new mayor needed someone who would be honest in his assessment of what would work and what wouldn't, and someone whom he could trust. Everett's first response was negative. Nutter then visited Everett and Elaine, and said to Elaine, "Everett needs to come with me, because there are two things I need as a politician: people I can trust around me, and someone I respect. Everett has lived a life that I respect. He's lived a life of his convictions. He's been clear about what he wants to do for people. He has had a calling to whatever he wants to put his hand towards, and I need him with me." The mayor won Elaine over.

Everett's entry into this new area of public service was a baptism of fire. He remembers that when he started "the police hated my guts. They assumed that because I represented people who kill police officers, that I would kill police officers." Yet, by the end of his time as Deputy Mayor, eight years later, relations had turned around, and the police were praising Everett for helping them to take a more community-based, holistic approach to dealing with crime. He cultivated constructive relationships with both the Police Commissioner and the police union leaders, and worked with both to achieve consensus. Everett relates, "We always butted heads, but we did it respectfully."

Given the weight and challenge of this new responsibility, the Mayor and Everett made a rule of praying before and after the making of decisions. They would say to each other, "we're just a couple of guys from West Philly, who are trying to do the right thing." Nutter would remind Everett that the "litmus test" was not, "what is the most expedient thing to do?" but "what do you believe is the right thing to do?" Mayor Nutter would later tell people that Everett brought a solid sense of being "grounded." Nutter says, "I was looking at a guy who exuded a connection to something bigger than ourselves."

Everett sums up his own approach: "I deliberate. I pray. Things happen." When he left public office in 2016, Everett was approached by his priest and asked to go back on Vestry. Everett at first turned him down. He really wanted to become a CEMD Christian again. However, his rector persisted, and Everett agreed, and then found himself appointed senior warden. Soon after, the rector announced that he was taking a position at another church. Everett was left in charge of Holy Apostles and the Mediator, a position he retains to this day.

Reflecting on his experiences and unique path through life, Everett acknowledges that, "at the times when I was at my lowest, the guiding light was there, even when I only had an inkling that Jesus was present in my life." He lives with a sense of loss, in that "People have poured themselves into me, in different ways. But most of them have now passed on [including the friend with whom he had attended Seminary]. Loss has always been a part of my life. It's almost like, as soon as I understand what a person's role is in my life, I lose them."

On the subject of calling, Everett says, "Responding to the call, whatever that call is in your life, sets you in a reflective mood at the same time that you are trying to stay present. And that duality is something that you feel intensely, as you are doing the things you are doing. And sometimes, it's very lonely."

At the church, Everett introduced the practice of praying the Daily Office. He explains, "If we start the day with prayer, and we end the day with prayer, at least we're giving ourselves the opportunity for God to say, 'I know what you went through today. I know that it was difficult. But seek ye first the kingdom of God.'"

Through Everett's leadership, the church has established partnerships within the local community, offering space in the church for a variety of ministries, including daycare facilities, a family counseling service which provides for local people, a baptist church whose pastor is deeply ingrained in the anti-violence movement, a lending library, and a food ministry.

Towards the end of our conversation, I ask him if his "call" is still there? "Yes, it is," he says. "At the time, I completely missed my wife's feelings. I had to own that as a man, and I had to own that as a husband. She said, 'You say that you're listening to people that really matter, and you heard nothing from me, and you didn't even miss my voice.' And that was very painful, and it remains very painful."

However, for Everett, the call to ordained ministry remains. When he mentioned to former Mayor and friend Michael Nutter that he was again thinking of following the path to ordained ministry, Nutter responded by saying that Everett's ministry is "actually being a voice in a room where usually it's never there. You will be there."

Nutter was referring to Everett's current work in the Defender's Office for the City of Philadelphia. Nutter describes his ministry as representing 1.6 million people "in the Administration. It will be for a lot of the people you call 'your guys.' The guys who are forgotten about, the guys who sometimes, yes, kill. The guys who do really bad things to others. But you sit with them. You get them to reflect. You get them to stop and think and maybe it's not always successful, but you've reached a lot of guys."

It is not only the fact that he is able to talk with and encourage his clients to re-evaluate their lives. Everett is himself an example of someone who has "a core which is true." In the same way that a priest is a sign of God's presence among us, so the person of integrity has an impact on all those whom they meet.

Everett's story underlines the basic understanding of "calling", which is to serve another in need. Answering a call means to serve another—God and the person in need. There is no guarantee that the need being addressed will be met completely, or that it will not continue. But in the world's hunger for love and compassion, there are always spaces where a person may enter and make a difference. God leaves these spaces open and visible, and a society's spiritual health may be measured by the responses of those who answer the call to serve, and who do so lovingly and sacrificially.

Everett's wife Elaine observes that at Holy Apostles and the Mediator, where there is a vacancy for a priest, Everett has, by necessity, assumed some of the priest's responsibilities. She says, "You preach on Sunday [at morning prayer], you do this writing ministry [of sending regular message to the congregation by email], you take care of the church—what's so different about what you're doing now, than if you were a priest?"

At the present time, the church is preparing to seek the services of a new rector. It is a challenging assignment, since there are fewer candidates than there were, even ten years ago. The new rector will need a strong sense of his or her own calling to serve effectively here. In the meantime, Everett is faithfully leading the church through the long period of transition. Having started the job, he will see the church through to the arrival of their new leader. And then? Listen for God's call, and ask God to open one door at a time.

CHAPTER 18

Ruth

The Call to Trust

On the morning of July 29, 1974, at the Church of the Advocate in Philadelphia, eleven women were ordained as priests in the Episcopal Church of America. The ordinations marked a radical change in the church's practice. The women had been ordained by bishops in good standing with the church, and thus their ordinations were valid. However, there was one snag: the church had never authorized women to be admitted to the priesthood. Thus, the ordinations had no legal standing.

It was only three years later, when the church voted to change the law, that all eleven women were fully acknowledged as priests.

News of the "Philadelphia Eleven", as they were known, made headlines across the country. The ordinations created serious divisions within the church. Some said that the church had no mandate to ordain women to the priesthood—to do so would violate the apostolic tradition as handed down over the centuries. Others disagreed, arguing that women priests would bring gifts that would benefit the church and the world.

Mary Helen Lawson, a former student of Yale Divinity school and mother of five children, read about the ordinations in the New York Times. She showed the paper to her 12 year old daughter Ruth and told her, "Now you can be what you want to be."

The call to priestly ministry was one that Ruth had had since she was five years old. Her father, the Rev. Peter Lawson, was a charismatic preacher who had been Dean of the Cathedral at Indianapolis when Ruth was growing up. Ruth soaked up the atmosphere of church and applied it to her home life. She remembers imitating the rituals of liturgy at home, re-purposing a large cloak closet as a holy place, and bringing her dolls there to be "baptized." The household cats, too, were baptized, because, as Ruth recalls, "that's what you do." She also remembers a party her parents hosted. An adult friend of her parents asked the five-year-old what she wanted to be when she grew up. "A priest," she replied, with absolute certainty. Her desire to be a priest was nothing more than a dream, since at the time there were no women priests. Nor were there women acolytes, ushers, lectors, or eucharistic ministers. The adult who listened to Ruth's reply laughed, but Ruth found the laughter perturbing. Why shouldn't she be a priest?

Growing up as the youngest in a family with four siblings, Ruth learned to differentiate herself early on. All the children shared in domestic duties, whether cleaning or cooking for the family. From the age of 11, she began earning money as a babysitter. She also earned money from singing in the choir. She learned to be self-sufficient, and her quick intelligence and talent for organizing others made her a formidable prospect for her Sunday school teachers. She admits today that she "would not have liked to have had me in Sunday School." "You need to behave!" was the cry of her teacher, whose class, involving the sticking of cotton balls onto the shape of a sheep, bored Ruth to tears. She much preferred being in church, especially in the choir, where she loved to sing.

Music has played an important role in Ruth's life, as a way of expressing her love for God. When she was young, her mother would use the lines on the oven as a stave, as a way of teaching her daughter to read music.

The choirmaster Jim Litton tells the story of another party at home when Ruth asked to join the Girls Choir. Mr. Litton explained,

"Well, Ruthie, you're not old enough yet."

"How old do I have to be?" she asked.

"You have to be eight."

"Why do I have to be eight?"

"That's how old choristers are when they start. Then you can read."

"But I can read now!"

Mr. Litton said that her charm and persistence won him over (as well as the fact that she was the dean's daughter.) Ruth was admitted as a six-turning-seven-year-old chorister. She spent eleven years in the girls' choir, where she loved the discipline of the choir, the rehearsals, and the camaraderie.

Not surprisingly, Ruth was as determined to be confirmed as she was to join the choir. The normal age was 12, but Ruth didn't see why she had to wait. Her father allowed her to attend confirmation class early, and she was confirmed at the age of 9. The tradition was for girls to wear veils on their heads, but Ruth said she didn't understand why girls had to and boys didn't. She made a stand by refusing to wear a veil and the rest of the girls in the confirmation class followed suit. All were confirmed *sans* veils.

When she was 11 years old, Ruth's father resigned as Dean of the Cathedral. A difference in political opinion with conservative opponents from within the congregation brought about the resignation of the liberal cleric. As a consequence, Ruth's parents stopped going to church. It was a major jolt to the family. All the children were offered the choice of staying at church or leaving. Ruth felt conflicted because of her loyalty to her father. However, in the end, she was resolved to continue going. "I have a ministry.

I'm not stopping church. I love the church. Church is my place, not just my dad's place." Ruth, along with three of her siblings, continued to attend.

Another shock came three years later when Ruth's parents decided to separate. It was a challenging time, and throughout this period Ruth received support from her siblings, school friends, and church friends. As her faith was being tested, her gifts and natural authority began to emerge. At the age of 15, she started teaching Sunday school to 3, 4, and 5-year-olds. In college, she taught a high school class. Her call remained strong, as did her love for the church. In fact, there was never a time in her life when she stopped attending church.

When she finished high school and entered college, Ruth was thinking ahead to the day when she would be a candidate at a seminary. The bishop supported and encouraged her call; however, his policy was against sending people to seminary straight from college. He said that Ruth should take a year out before entering seminary.

Ruth takes up the story.

> *I had been working in the Welfare Department in the Aid to Dependent Children Division, in Monroe County when I was at university. It was part of my work-study job, as I worked myself through university and I was a file clerk there, but I thought I could do wha t those caseworkers do. So, I took the test and passed with a score that allowed me to be an investigative caseworker in Child Protection Services. I started that job in the fall of '83 and saw the degradation and the violence and the meanness of poverty and of bad parenting. I saw children burned and cut and bruised. That tested me. I asked, 'Why is there so much sin and violence in a place that is supposed to be loving?'*

After a year at the Welfare Department, Ruth was interviewed by the Bishop's Advisory Committee on Admission to Ministry (BACAM) as a possible candidate for seminary. On paper, she had impressive credentials. She was a faithful and lifelong churchgoer. She had led retreats on Christian education for the choir. She was on the Diocesan Youth Council, contributing to Youth programs within the diocese. She says, "People responded to my leadership." To attend the meeting with BACAM, she had to skip the beginning of a retreat for Youth leaders. At the end of the interview, she headed back to the retreat. Shortly afterward, she received a phone call. The Committee had decided not to recommend her for seminary. Ruth says she was "dumbfounded." The BACAM declined to give a reason for their decision but told her to come back in a year's time. During this period, she was to meet with a "shepherd"—an ordained clergyperson—and also undergo group counseling.

Ruth reached out to the "shepherd," but received no response. She also attended the group counseling sessions, as directed, but after three sessions the leader told her, "You don't really need to be here." Ruth stopped attending group therapy. Meanwhile, she continued to work at the Welfare Department. She was transferred from a physical abuse and neglect unit to the Special Unit, addressing child sexual abuse. She remembers, "Now I am 23 years old, and investigating incest, cases where children are sexually abused."

After another year she applied again to be considered for ordained ministry, but the Bishop's Advisory Committee thought Ruth was being disobedient in leaving therapy, and so declined her application a second time. There was no advice about what she should do next. It was the spring of '85. All Ruth could think of to do was to visit the Dean of the Cathedral, who then contacted the Bishop. The message got back to Ruth that she should attend individual therapy, since the perception was that she was trying to fix her father's failed ministry. One further stipulation: she had to leave the cathedral. This was the hardest requirement, since the cathedral was her spiritual home, and the only church she had known.

As a consequence, Ruth had to stop youth ministry and leave the cathedral singing group. She recalls this period in her life as a "wilderness time." She spent a year wandering from parish to parish, "seeing what churches were like." However, she was allowed to maintain a weekly contact with the cathedral, as the bishop invited Ruth to acolyte for him at the 7:00 am Tuesday eucharist.

Prior to her third meeting with the BACAM, Ruth had, along with another prospective candidate, started helping out at a homeless shelter once a week. She was still working full time for the Welfare department. She had shown obedience to the Bishop's Advisory Committee by seeing a therapist and by leaving the cathedral. During her interview with BACAM, she was asked if she was trying to heal her father's ministry and make it right. Ruth answered, "I can't do that, and I'm not called to that. I'm called to my own ministry." The committee finally gave her the green light to go to seminary. Ruth always wondered if the Dean and Bishop had in some way influenced BACAM's decision.

Ruth entered Virginia Theological Seminary in the fall of '86 and graduated in the spring of '89. She chose VTS because of its long evangelical tradition and emphasis on missionary work. Her experience at seminary was mixed. She enjoyed the class work and the regular discipline of daily chapel. Talking with professors and discussing the finer points of theology increased her understanding of the faith. She was elected president of the student body because, she says now, "I organized good parties." On the down side, a number of her colleagues were opposed to women as priests. They expressed their disapproval by absenting themselves from chapel, when the associate dean, who was the first woman priest on the staff, was presiding at the eucharist. While Ruth accepted their right to hold different views, she thinks that their disrespectful behavior in this and on other occasions did them no credit. It remains an abiding question for the church: how can we live with our differences without violating the spirit of charity that is fundamental to Christian life and witness?

Upon leaving the seminary, Ruth was curate at St. Paul's, Chestnut Hill, and then became the Rector of St. Peter's in Glenside, Pennsylvania, a position she held for 13 years. In 2007 she applied for the position of Rector at Christ Church Christiana Hundred, Wilmington, Delaware, and the largest Episcopal Church in the diocese of Delaware. She was accepted and continues to live out her call there to this day.

This book is dedicated to Ruth, a loving and gifted preacher, teacher, and pastor. Ruth also happens to be my wife, and we have been married since 2016. Writing about one's other half has advantages and disadvantages. The first advantage is that if I need to check a detail or ask a follow up question, Ruth is there to answer it for me. The chief disadvantage is that I am not impartial. Having said that, in my defense I would say that more people than I can count have said to me privately how much they appreciate my wife's ministry and care for them. When I was Rector at Church of the Redeemer, Springfield, Pennsylvania, one of my parishioners remembered Ruth from long ago, and how she entered a church and lit up the place with her joy and enthusiasm. Her faithfulness to God, and God's faithfulness to her, has given her a kind of divine confidence. This confidence isn't one that comes from pride, but is grounded in genuine humility.

Can one's calling change over time? Ruth says, "I don't think [my call] has changed but over the years at various time, different aspects of the priestly vocation have risen to the forefront. Sometimes I am more of a pastor, or more of a teacher, or more of an administrator and organizer." There was another call which came her way and that was the call to be a bishop. In 2003 Ruth entered into the selection process for bishop of New Hampshire. This was an opportunity for Ruth's gifts of organizing, uniting and inspiring congregations to be expressed in a diocese as a whole, rather than in one church. However, in the final count, the nomination went to the Rt. Rev. Gene Robinson, with Ruth coming in second. For Ruth, the result was disappointing. It raised questions in her mind about the extent of her own calling. She asked herself, "What am I called to be? Am I called to be a bishop? I know I am called to serve the Church. I know I am called to priesthood."

Looking back, Ruth sees how God continues to work through her and her priestly calling. She says, "As I've aged, being the pastor, the local presence in a church—I mean, just hearing from a person, I knew their mother, I know them—something the church has lost, as we've picked up people and moved them from place to place, is the faithfulness that endures, that binds us together."

There were other calls essential to Ruth's life, including motherhood. It isn't easy juggling the needs of home and parish, as any priest who is married with children can tell you. There are particular emotional and spiritual demands placed on clergy which make the role more challenging than most people realize. It takes a rare combination of sensitivity and stamina to hold everything together.

Central to the life of a Christian is the person's relationship with Jesus. Ruth identifies with two Bible characters who express, in a way, Ruth's own relationship with Jesus. The first is Peter, the Church's first leader. In self-deprecatory manner, Ruth sums up in two words what she and Peter have in common. "Brash and quick," she says.

The other Bible character with whom Ruth identifies is Jairus's daughter. (Mark 5:21-43) Ruth explains: "Jesus has taken me by the hand and raised me up, healed me and given me life. It's not necessarily 'healing' in the way of sickness to healing, or sickness to wholeness, but in weakness to strength, from flagging zeal to a sense of possibility and life. When Jesus takes me by the hand, I can do all things through him who strengthens me. When I am not holding his hand—when he's not raising me up—I can't serve, I can't raise up. So, that story has great power for me, in reminding me that I am only strong when he is with me."

The call to love informs the whole of the life of a priest—or any Christian, for that matter. But how is love to be expressed? One of the books which attempts to answer this question is *The Risk of Love*, by the Church of England vicar W. H. Vanstone. It was influential in Ruth's own formation as a priest. The book was published in the United States under a different title: *Love's Endeavor, Love's Expense*. Ruth summarizes the book's own impact on her:

Love works in its mysterious way to carry out its purpose. God's love is for us and in us and through us. The endeavor of love is self-offering, self-sacrifice, and that's also its expense; it costs something to love. And yet, to not give love, to not expend love in this world would be impoverishing both to me and to God, who has given so generously and immensely—this gift of life and his love in Jesus Christ for the world.

On a final note, Ruth looks at the nature of her own call and how it can only be expressed through God who is the origin and fullest expression of love. She says, "God's love for me—to know God's blessing that means God's love for me. To know that God desires my joy in this life and in the life to come. Aligning myself in some way to find that, is my work of love for God and for others. So, yes, the call is to love with all my gifts and all my faults in all ways that I can."

Epilogue

Recently I had lunch with a former parishioner, who used to prepare the weekly parish email. We hadn't seen each other for a while, so our meeting was an opportunity for a catch-up. Over lunch she informed me that she had left the church where we had once both worshiped and was now attending another church. I asked her how it was going. She said it was difficult at first, but that she was learning to adapt and make new friends. I was sorry to hear about her leaving, but then remembered that God can sometimes call us out of one place and into another.

She told me a story about an elderly couple she knew but hadn't seen for years. She said that their names kept coming up in her prayers, and so she decided to call them. The wife answered the call and said that her husband had just gone into hospital for an emergency procedure: quadruple heart bypass surgery. My friend then realized why the couple was in her thoughts. God needed her to offer support at a critical time. I told her that I was writing a book on how God calls people to serve in the church and the world. At the end of lunch she gave me a birthday present which I opened when I got home. It was a small book titled *Jesus Calling*. It was one of those serendipitous moments when you say, "Uh-oh, how did she know that?"

I began writing this book before I left my last call as interim rector. That assignment had ended abruptly and unexpectedly and had raised questions in my own mind about my own call to ordained ministry. The past year has been one of uncertainty, as I entered my own "wilderness" time.

I learned to live in a state of semi-chaos, at least as far as my own vocation is concerned, and to "go with the flow." I continued to search for work where I could find it. I took funerals. I did supply work, which brought me into wonderful churches I would never have visited before, mainly in Philadelphia. I led study courses at three different churches in Wilmington, Delaware. Unexpectedly, I joined the 5 p.m. service on Saturday at Christ Church Christiana Hundred as a guitarist and sometimes bassist. In between, I continued working on this book. In many ways, the writing of the book has been therapeutic.

I mentioned in an earlier chapter about the importance of accepting the call to change, and to that I can add the call to *adapt*. God calls us to do things we weren't expecting to do, and those earlier lessons about listening and responding are in my mind as I navigate the "chaos" of my current situation. I am reminded of something that the late Father Gregory, from the monastic community of which I am an associate, once said to me: "God will be faithful to your calling."

I am grateful to all those who have encouraged me to complete the book. My purpose in writing it is to show how God calls us wherever and whoever we are, and that God guides and supports those who offer themselves in his service. Answering God's call draws us into the mystery of life, where personal fulfillment is found, not in seeking one's own good, but the good of others. It means to live the gospel life, of which Jesus is both the author and the example.

It can be a wild adventure at times, while at other times the journey can be tranquil and unremarkable. In all situations, God is present and is calling us beyond ourselves to see the limitless possibilities above the horizon. May God bless you and give you ears as you listen for God's call to you.

About the Author

David Beresford is currently the interim rector of the Episcopal Church of the Messiah, in Gwynedd, Pennsylvania. He was ordained in the Church of England in 2009, and moved to the USA in 2016. In 2022, he was awarded an MA in Theology from the University of Chichester. He trained as a Spiritual Director and has designed and led a number of faith-based courses. He is the author of *Above & Below*, and lives in Wilmington, Delaware, with his wife Ruth and their cat Mani.

Colophon

Call to Love was designed in Italy by Bob Schwartz on an Apple MacPro using Adobe InDesign and Photoshop CC. The book title is set in 70 point Ross Antique Roman. Chapter titles and sub-titles were set in 41 point and 24 point Gabrielle, respectively. Primary text was set in twelve-point Iowan Old Style, fourteen-point leaded. The front and back material titles were set in 14-point Iowan Old Style and the text was set in ten-point Adelle sans, thirteen-point leaded.

Ross Antique Roman is a classic period font designed by John Studden. It is named after Ross F. George, and based on a style from George's 1929 *Speedball Text Book*.

Gabrielle is a script, calligraphy font designed by the German typographer, Dieter Steffmann.

Iowan Old Style—designed by John Downer and released by Bitstream in 1991—is inspired by serif typefaces from Renaissance Italy, now called the "old-style" or Venetian model of typeface design, with influence from Downer's work as hand-painter of signs.

Adelle Sans—the sans serif counterpart to the award-winning Adelle type family—was designed by Veronika Burian and José Scaglione of the TypeTogether foundry.

www.ingramcontent.com/pod-product-compliance
Lightning Source LLC
Chambersburg PA
CBHW051314120626
46547CB00015B/2236